A Month of Summers

A Month of Summers

by

Ian Scott

photography by Campbell
and James MacCallum

TERENCE DALTON LIMITED
LAVENHAM • SUFFOLK
1994

Published by
TERENCE DALTON LIMITED

ISBN 0 86138 104 1

*Printed in Great Britain at
The Lavenham Press Limited, Lavenham, Suffolk*

Contents

Foreword

I have spent a good part of the last thirty years writing. Often—particularly in the early years—in the early morning, sometimes the very early morning that comes soon after very late at night. And at night. Until my pen has developed a will of its own and I have hauled myself to bed.

Often in the succession of offices that have been my workday homes. At the World Bank in Washington DC and in Bogota, Colombia; at the United Nations in Bogota, and in Santo Domingo in the Dominican Republic; at the International Coffee Organization in London; and at the University of Durham, where I learned, more than twenty-five years ago, that I did not, after all, want to be an academic.

Often at home. In the early years, at a desk with steel legs and a simulated teak top, which I bought in Newcastle in 1968 because it gave me the largest workspace for the money I could then afford to spend. In later years, and now, at a wonderful, old, dark work table—which lists slightly to port, and bears the scars of stories I should love to hear—that we bought in 1978 at Puente Nacional, in the Department of Boyaca, Colombia, about six hours' drive from the capital city that now celebrates both its colonial and its republican traditions in the name of Santa Fe de Bogota.

The things I have been writing about all this time have, for the most part, captured my imagination and turned my brain into a rabbit warren of serious enquiry. With the exception of a book about urbanization in Mexico about ten years ago, and some professional articles, almost everything I have written has had a single purpose: to help international institutions make sound decisions. About where to allocate their resources. About which economic policies to endorse. And, in the last ten years, about how the World Bank should manage its internal affairs. It would be untrue to say I have enjoyed writing everything I have written, but I certainly count myself exceedingly fortunate to have been able to spend my time doing what I have done.

At the same time, I find the idea of writing something that has no other purpose than to entertain both shocking and alluring, a frivolous indulgence and a forbidden fruit. The prospect of escaping from the rules of evidence, from the overwhelming need to be objective, from the careful weighing of options, is seductive. The chance to define relevance in terms of what I think is relevant, to use information selectively, to write about my feelings, is like Christmas morning, sacking a candy store, and eating and drinking without constraint, all together.

This is, so to speak, my second coming to North Norfolk this year. The first time was only for what amounted to a long weekend, which improbably combined Carey's graduation from Cambridge, our wedding anniversary, Carey's birthday, and my mother's birthday—all in the space of three days. Then, back to Washington to finish some urgent work. And now I am here for a whole month without a serious threat that I shall have to go back to Washington in the middle of my holiday.

Glynis says the weather has been off colour for the last fortnight. But today, the sun is shining. And while I know it will take me several days to unwind—it always does, and this year it will probably take longer than usual—I am already beginning to relax, as the memories of thirty other summers since I first came to Norfolk begin to warm my mind and the sights and sounds and smells of this place blend again in a seamless tapestry of golden impressions.

I let my senses wander. And they create a collage: of July wheat and barley, nearly but not quite ready for harvest; purple carpets of just-bloomed sea lavender on the saltmarshes; sharp reflections of sunlight on pools of seawater abandoned by the ebbing tide; the comfortable groan of wood on wood as the gaff settles on the new tack; springy, spongy grass on the narrow greens that separate the saltmarsh from arable land; the incessant chatter of oyster-catchers disturbed on the foreshore; the crumbling remnants of concrete runways among sugar beet fields where Stirlings and Wellingtons and Mosquitoes, laden with destruction, once trundled to take off; the ancient and impossibly beautiful symbols of the Anglican Church that decorate the landscape; the newer and impossibly ugly symbols of Nonconformity it would be architecturally better off without; the twin boom of the maroon that tells the crew of Wells lifeboat somebody is in peril on the North Sea; the contrast between the look-alike dunes, covered with dense scrub and Corsican pines, that separate the famous fields reclaimed by Coke of Holkham in the eighteenth century from the vast beach that slopes imperceptibly to the water's edge at low tide; the feeling one is visiting a museum in the pub at Burnham Thorpe that looks much the same today as it did when Horatio Nelson, the rector's son, might have been a regular...

The list is not endless but I could certainly go on and on. I won't, because something tells me an inventory of sensations that are precious to me, and that may stir reactions in others who know North Norfolk, may have less appeal out of context to those who do not, and that it would be better to save some for use in what I shall write in the course of the next month.

At this juncture, I have no idea whether I shall find a publisher, or whether people will want to read what I write. But having let the idea of writing this book marinate in my mind for more than a decade, I now feel compelled to discover how my intense emotions about this place will take shape on paper. In fact, I can hardly wait to read what I am going to write.

July 1992

Dedication

For Alison, Campbell, Catherine, Christine,
Dick, Dorothy, Gary, Jenny, Marion, Miranda, Rex, Richard,
Rodney, Sheila and Wilfred;

And for Carey, Caitlin, Catriona and Cameron;

And of course for Glynis.

Thanks

To Campbell MacCallum whose images grace my words;
Elisabeth Whitehair, Director of Terence Dalton, who has
been a delight to work with; Mavourneen Cox, who smoothed
the rough edges of my typescript; and the unknown
thousands who love North Norfolk as much as I do and,
in their own ways, preserve the Magic Kingdom.

20 July

Glynis has abandoned me. But only for two weeks while she is off in Oxford doing a course on international education. Rather her than me. So I shall have the younger children all to myself. Delightful. At least for me, because I spend so much of my time in Washington at the Bank, and because when I am at home there are so many things to do in the house and garden that I don't see nearly as much of them there as I'd like to. And these childhood years are so soon over. It seems only a year or so ago—it is actually nearly twenty —that Carey and Caitlin were running in and out of our house, covered in marsh mud, playing fantasy games, and going down to the village shop that is really called Howells' but which we have always called Wally's because one of the first things Carey learned to read was the big Walls ice-cream sign outside it. And now Carey has finished at Pembroke and has gone off to Moscow to earn her living for the first time. And Caitlin has decided not to spend the summer here in Norfolk but back in Washington because that is a bigger contrast with Scotland where she has spent the last academic year and will spend the next three.

No schedule. No objectives. No appointments. No meetings. Vive la difference! I wondered at the time why a German colleague who is now a very senior manager in the Bank looked at me as though I were mad when I told him, some years ago, that the first thing I did when I got to Norfolk was to draw up a schedule of places to go and things to do in the course of our holiday. With alternatives, of course, should the weather prevent us from doing what was originally scheduled.

'We've got to work hard at having a good time,' I used to say. And then I'd mutter things like, 'Time and tide wait for no man'; or, 'High water was half an hour ago and we're not even down to the slipway yet'; or, 'Why bother with washing up, we're wasting a good day and it might rain tomorrow, so let's go'. I'm lucky I still have a wife and four children. Even luckier they still want to come to Norfolk as much as I do.

One good thing though: because we did work so hard for so many summers at getting to know the nooks and crannies—I wonder by the way, if I would know a cranny if I saw one—of North Norfolk, we really got to know it intimately, better probably than many of our friends who live here all the time. For them, there is always tomorrow, or next week, or next year. But the days pass and the weeks pass and the years become decades and they still haven't been to many of the places we have been to. It's always like that, I suppose. For the same reason, I have never visited the White House, although for most of the last twenty years I have had an office only a block away. And when I lived in London for twenty years I never went to things like the Trooping of the Colour until visitors suggested going. It is quite likely I will wake up one day as I near retirement and departure from Washington and realize, in panic, that there are dozens of things to do that I have not done and places to go that I have not been to. But then I don't feel quite the same way about Washington as I feel about North Norfolk.

I wonder, is it just laziness or indifference that causes us to leave places unseen and things undone? Is it also, at least in part, because people who live in magical places all the time don't want to be mistaken for visitors? Is it what makes people put bumper stickers on their cars on the island of Martha's Vineyard announcing they are Natives?

How to share what—I fondly imagine—are my insights about this place? By writing a guide book? As they say in the United States, 'No way!' By keeping a detailed diary ? As Cameron would say, 'I don't think so!' Perhaps I should start by defining my terms, my subject matter and, if I can decide what they are, my motives.

The Magic Kingdom

Some years ago, we spent several summer vacations on the island of Martha's Vineyard off the coast of Massachusetts. One of the man-made wonders of that island, which is extraordinarily rich in natural beauty, was its bi-weekly newspaper, the *Vineyard Gazette*. Another was its erstwhile editor, Henry Beetle Hough. Besides creating what is widely recognized as one of the best newspapers of its kind, Henry Beetle Hough wrote more than a dozen books. Ostensibly they were about the Vineyard. But they were in fact no more about Martha's Vineyard than *Macbeth* is about betrayal or *King Lear* is about disloyalty. Undoubtedly, however, they were inspired by the Vineyard.

It was reading and re-reading Hough's work that gave me the idea, some years ago now, that I might be inspired to write about a place that I know and love—in much the same way, I think, that he loved the Vineyard. I could measure neither his wit nor his wisdom. But I thought I might try my hand at interpreting my Magic Kingdom in something like the same way that Hough, who died on the Vineyard in 1987, interpreted his Magic Kingdom for me and others who knew, from the moment they set foot on his enchanted island, that they had arrived in a special place and were hungry to unlock its secrets.

I am convinced there are Magic Kingdoms everywhere. How else to explain the urge to go home, to a place as well as to people? How else to explain why my wife's grandfather, having lived for sixty of his eighty years in my Magic Kingdom of North Norfolk, felt compelled to return to his Magic Kingdom, a dingle on the borders of what were then Denbighshire and Shropshire, where he wanted to die? Magic Kingdoms exist, I believe, because human beings have an innate capacity to develop loving relationships with places as well as with other people.

The love of places, like the love of people, inspires fierce emotion; people lie down in the paths of bulldozers to preserve loved fragments of landscape. It generates boundless energy; petitions are signed by thousands to protect wetlands, woodlands, and heaths from development. It stimulates political action of a high order; witness the successful battle fought by the collective lovers of Martha's Vineyard to keep McDonalds (and in practice all their competitors) off the island in the mid 1970s. And it produces extraordinary generosity in the form of donations and bequests, usually to keep things as they are—if not for ever, for as long as possible.

For some of us, these relationships are monogamous. An accident of birth, and loyalty is defined for ever. For some, it happens through adoption—in childhood or adulthood—and the love may be the more passionate because the roots are grafted. For the promiscuous, life is a succession of one loved place after another. Just as there are those who cannot meet a physically attractive new person without falling in love with him or her, there are those who cannot visit an attractive new place without wanting to possess a piece of it; within hours of the first encounter they rush to the local realtor or, if in Britain, the estate agent. For the polygamous, the love of one place remains firm, but not exclusive; hence the seasonal migrations between Florida and New England and between Provence and Old England. And then, of course, there are the romantics—or perhaps it is the romantic side of all of us—dreaming impossible dreams of places never visited and experiencing unrequited lust for untrodden soil. Sometimes the dream comes true, only to shatter illusions that might better have remained illusions. Few things are sadder than the traveller who should have stayed at home. Or the retiree who has known a place in the charmed light of summer and finds it has another side when winter comes; just as the beautiful woman met at night is something else in the harsh light of morning.

For me, North Norfolk is quite simply the most magical place on Earth. And my allegiance to it is unconditional. But there are other places in which I have lived or worked, or that I have visited for shorter or longer periods, to which I also owe allegiance. Of a different order, to be sure, but I love them too. The Chesapeake Bay country of Maryland and Virginia is one of them. Martha's Vineyard another. The Sabana de Bogota, in Colombia, yet another.

And I have a romantic fascination with a place to which I have never been and know only from a set of black-and-white photographs I saw one evening in 1969 in the Spanish Embassy in Santo Domingo. All this time I have been desperately hoping that when, eventually, I go there, it will be as magical as I remember it. A couple of years ago when Carey and Caitlin were travelling in Spain, I asked them to go to the town of Trujillo in the province of Caceres in Extremadura, and to tell me what it was like when they returned. They told me it was hot and dull and lifeless and that I must be out of my mind to think I would love it. No matter. I am still devoted, and I am sure they missed what I am looking for. Next year, perhaps, we shall go there on the way to or from Norfolk. Or perhaps we shan't. Perhaps we shall find a reason not to go there, thus ensuring the image of high walls rising from a dry and sun-soaked plain remains intact. I suppose the parallels between human love and the love of places can be overdone but I find them palpable.

Most of the places I love are rural. But in all of them, human hands have left strong impressions. I have been awed—isn't everyone who sees them?—by the natural magnificence of the Grand Canyon in Arizona; the Falls of Iguazu where Argentina, Brazil, and Paraguay meet; and the deserts of what were, at the time I first saw them, still called the Trucial States. But human impressions are tentative in such places. All too often one comes across the ruins of failed efforts to reach terms with them: a broken house here, a rusted vehicle there.

The places I love best have all been tamed but not entirely subdued. There is, in each of them, an element of risk. Small, but still present. Of giant storms and winter gales in North Norfolk. Of hurricanes on the Vineyard or in the Chesapeake Bay. Of flooding rains on the Sabana de Bogota. And (in my imagination) of searing white heat in Extremadura. Nature is there in all of these places.

But each of them also derives a fundamental part of its character from the villages and towns that punctuate landscapes and measure history. There are no cities. No suburban sprawl. Certainly no exurban creep.

I have nothing against cities. I have lived in them all my life. I spent my childhood in the Inner London suburb of what is now called Brent but was then called Willesden; strange, is it not, how a place can be renamed and a thousand years of history wiped out, just like that, even if the place is a grotty place like Willesden? And I have lived for the last twenty years in the delightful and leafy Washington suburb of McLean, Virginia—which has no history at all. But I suspect that places only live in one's heart if one can live in their hearts and that some places—like Willesden and McLean—do not have hearts to live in.

That, I think, is why commuting can be such a heartless proposition and also why people who are honest about other things almost always lie when asked about the duration of their journeys to and from work. The same people, by the way, may also be generous with the truth about certain other things, such as taking the green channel at airports when they should go through the red one; forgetting to return library books—or even books that belong to their friends; the frequency with which they exercise; and (if over 40) their real waist size.

But then, if your life is dominated by a railway timetable, there is an overwhelming temptation to fantasize. How else to cope with the reality of getting up in the dark, catching the train in the dark, travelling to the city in the dark, and then doing all that backwards at the end of the day? Voluntary amnesia, deliberately wiping out the four hours a day, twenty hours a week spent as the captive of British Rail or Amtrak or some other God-awful railway company is, after all, better than madness. Particularly if the place from and to which you commute is not lovable. Home could be a soulless piece of exurbia, created in the space of nine months on what used to be a wheat field?

I tried living in one of those places for a while in 1970. Returning to England from the Caribbean to work in London, we rented a house near Cambridge from friends. It was October when we arrived. The days got shorter. The mornings got darker. The evenings got darker still. I saw the house by daylight only at weekends. And what I saw had been carefully crafted by a crafty developer to give the impression that the houses had grown there organically, one at a time, instead of as bits of an architect's plan for an instant community. I suppose some people love places like that, but my feeling is that they are intrinsically unlovable.

Small towns and villages—real ones that have grown slowly over time, which you can cross on foot in fifteen minutes and where, after you have lived there a while, the strangers are the people you don't recognize—are easy to live in. I know there are people who claim to love New York. Or Paris. Or Rome. And other metropolitan places all over the world. But I think what they really love is small pieces of them, small enough to know intimately and thus to love. Love is intimacy, right? How could anyone, even the most active lover the world has ever known, love the whole of London? And even if you could, why would you want to? It may be old but that makes it neither enchanting nor entrancing.

The places in my heart all have cities within easy access of them; Norwich, Annapolis, Boston, Santa Fe de Bogota. But I find these cities special mainly because the Magic Kingdoms are there; without their hinterlands they would be unremarkable, at least to me. I dare say I would still think of Norwich—as its leading financial services business does—as a fine city even if North Norfolk were not there. But no more so than, say, Salisbury, or York or Canterbury. Likewise, it is the Chesapeake Bay that makes Annapolis special, the Vineyard that makes Boston significant, and the Altiplano that makes Bogota what it is.

Magic Kingdoms are finite. They have precise boundaries that may be visible, as those of island kingdoms are defined by their shores. But their boundaries may be invisible to those who cannot feel their magic. North Norfolk is like that. It is not East Anglia or even Norfolk as a whole that is magic. West Norfolk—a wasteland of flat, boggy, boring, fens that would have been better left in their medieval condition, and with ugly exposed houses and bottle-necked roads I can do without. If I never see King's Lynn again I shall not weep. And I shall go out of my way to avoid going anywhere near Great Yarmouth,which might have been quaint when Dickens wrote about it but strikes me now as a poor imitation of

Ocean City. And, coming closer to home, Cromer and Sheringham to the east, and Hunstanton—which is always pronounced 'Hunston' by people who do not know that Norfolk people say 'Hunstanton'—to the west, are all places I would much rather ignore. Which brings me, at last, to the question of definition: where is North Norfolk anyway?

A physical geographer will tell you it is partly defined by the North Alluvial Plain that stretches from Holme in the west to Weybourne in the east. The plain is a patchwork of freshwater marshes reclaimed from the North Sea, saltmarshes that have accumulated over a thousand years, and offshore islands, spits, and bars perpetually shaped and reshaped by wind and tide. There is no question that the alluvial plain is the essence of North Norfolk because its marshes—pristine or reclaimed—define it. Or that the towns and villages that lie comfortably behind it are made mysterious chiefly by their association with it or that their mystery is fed by what a philosopher friend of mine might call their facticity.

The marshes define the northern or seaward boundary of the Magic Kingdom. Where they begin it begins. And where they end it ends. But over the years the shoreline on my mental map of the Kingdom has perversely shifted several times. Like the tides, the western and eastern limits of the coast have moved in, then out. We explored the western edge: did it go all the way to Holme where the Peddars Way supposedly hit the coast? Did it include Titchwell and Thornham? Or Brancaster Town—as distinct from Brancaster Staithe, about which there was never a doubt?

To the east, the geographer suggests the Magic Kingdom might end at Weybourne. But then between Blakeney and Cley the beach turns to pebbles; is that a problem? And is Salthouse in or out, home turf or foreign soil? We eventually drew the boundary lines where we sensed they should be. Not in terms of precise and objective criteria, but in unapologetically subjective terms by which we decreed which places were included and which were excluded.

Our decision was that the coastline of the Magic Kingdom of North Norfolk begins at Brancaster Staithe—sorry, Thornham, you didn't quite make it... you could try those people over there; they're making a mental map of North Norfolk too and perhaps they could include you in their version—and ended in the east at Cley. Why? Simply because those were the boundaries that trial and error and sense and sensibility told us were the right boundaries.

Inland, the limits of the Kingdom are harder to define. And ultimately it is intuition that tells you where they are. At one time I thought it was simply a matter of distance from the coast. It is not.

There are some inland places that do belong, and others that do not. To a degree, it is local sensitivity to, and awareness of, the sea and the marshes that determine where is in and where is out. Little things, none particularly significant in itself. But each a tell-tale sign.

The inland boundary is not defined by what Arthur Young, in 1770, called the 'Good Sands' area. That extends too far inland. But the sands do indeed define the soils of the Magic Kingdom; they would not be magical without them. And so, where, in a landward direction, is it?

An approximate answer is provided by an arc that sweeps inland from Brancaster Staithe, through the Burnhams, embraces Fakenham, and sweeps up again to the coast at Cley. It thus includes a specific set of villages and excludes others. Those included are Brancaster Staithe and the seven Burnhams by the sea—which is to say Deepdale (which is contiguous with Brancaster Staithe), Westgate and Sutton (which together make up Burnham Market), Norton, Overy Town, Overy Staithe, and Thorpe. South of the Burnhams there are North and South Creake. East of the vast park that surrounds Holkham Hall you come to Wells, Warham, Wighton, Great and Little Walsingham (which inaccurately describes their relative sizes), Great and Little Snoring (which are roughly accurate descriptors), Egmere, the Barshams (East, North, and West, but no South), Hindringham, Binham, Langham, Cockthorpe, Morston, Blakeney, Stiffkey, and Cley.

I do not claim this is the right definition of North Norfolk. Only that it is right for me. If others wish to include Salthouse, that's absolutely fine. If their mental maps encompass Holt, I can see their point. I would not dream of arguing the toss on a question that does not have a right or a wrong answer. I only know that when I cross the invisible boundary that separates my Magic Kingdom from the rest of the world, my pulse quickens, my senses sharpen and I begin to feel a contentment that, for reasons I do not understand—and do not really need to understand—I have only ever felt there. Some years ago, a developer in Blakeney was selling time-share apartments, still a rather new concept in England though well known in America. He put up a sign saying: 'Peace for Sale'. Well, you obviously can't sell peace and you obviously can't buy it, and I thought it crass, or as Carey would say, 'naff'. But I knew exactly what he meant.

Although I do now not mind at all if other people think North Norfolk is somewhere else, and would not dream of competing with anybody to determine who knew North Norfolk best, or who loved it most, there was a time when I felt differently because love and jealousy sometimes get confused. I remember a dreadful

Sunday picnic on the dunes between Gun Hill and Holkham, when I spent a whole afternoon competing with a woman—who I later decided was perfectly sensible—about who had more local knowledge. I felt ashamed even while it was happening; more so afterwards. But I could not help myself at the time.

There was also a period when I was only willing to share the treasures of my Kingdom with special friends. And I was mortified if they did not react with awe when I showed them the awesome. I don't feel that way any more either, which is why, I suppose, having spent several years thinking about this book, I have finally started to write it.

Those who are fortunate enough to have fallen in love with a place can take you to a specific location that for them captures its soul and distils its essence. There is one such location in my Magic Kingdom: the centre of its universe. Yet when I take friends there—as I sometimes do—and tell them they are, so to speak, in a cathedral, they are always polite but usually do not get the point. Are they embarrassed?

There are long views to east and west across the marshes to the smudges of two coastal villages. The sea is far away to the north because the tide is out and this place can only be reached on foot at low tide. There is a lot of sky, which may be filled with clouds of white candy-floss or with grey streaks that threaten rain. It would be hard to find a less dramatic landscape or one with fewer features. Few of the hundreds of water-colourists and painters who are thick on the ground in the Magic Kingdom have thought to paint it, although one of them, a full-time fisherman and part-time painter, did so thirty years ago on a dull October morning. I am grateful to him and grateful to Glynis who bought his painting for me as a Christmas present the year before we were married. It hangs in our bedroom in McLean.

So the task I have set myself is to explain why and how I love this country. And my example is Henry Beetle Hough's explanation of why and how he loved Martha's Vineyard. This is not a guidebook. Nor a recipe book of things to do and places to go for the use of explorers. If I am to define it at all, it is an interpretation of what, for me, is a unique place and an attempt—in which I truthfully hope to be no more than partially successful because I really don't want Tom or Dick or Harry to invade it—to fashion, with words, a master key that unlocks the doors of the Magic Kingdom. Some of them, that is.

25 July

The children have gone to bed. They both fell asleep watching the opening ceremony of the Olympics from Barcelona. Amazing. Especially the arrow that lit the flame. Suppose he had missed!

It seems as though the only time I shall get to write is before breakfast or after dinner. At this rate I shan't get much done. But no matter. I have time. Probably more time in the month I spend here than in the rest of the year put together. In which to do as I will, or rather, as I will, subject to the wills of Cameron and Catriona and, when she gets back, Glynis.

One thing is quite clear already. I can only write this book here. So what doesn't get written in the next nearly–a–month will not get done at all. Last time we were here I made some tapes on a micro-recorder with the intention of using them to write when I got back to Washington. They are still in the drawer in my work table, and I have never touched them; emotion recollected in tranquillity doesn't work for me. At least, not for this purpose.

My guess is I shall do enough to complete a manuscript and then I shall have the agony of putting it all on a word processor when I get back to Washington. (Note: Washington, 2 September 1992, Agony? I was out of my skull when I wrote that. This is much worse than agony. I've been trying for the last half-hour to merge two pieces I transcribed at the weekend and the damn thing keeps telling me I've got a disc error.)

The trees in the courtyard outside are bending over and shaking in the wind. Perhaps we'll go sailing on tomorrow morning's tide. And perhaps we won't.

Like a Well-Tuned Cello

When I tell people in America I have two boats in England—I always say England because few of them have heard of Norfolk and even fewer have been there—I speak truth. Almost. Because I then rush on to say that the biggest of them is not quite twenty feet from stem to stern—well, actually, I don't say that, I just say twenty feet long, but that is what I would say if I wanted to speak correct boatspeak—and that I only own half of it and my brother-in-law owns the other half. Then I tell them the second one is only twelve feet long. And that both of them were bought for a song. Not literally, thank God, because at school I achieved the rare distinction of being invited to leave the school orchestra (in which I played the trumpet sadistically badly) and join the choir, but I was so awful there they told me to go back to the orchestra. But the fact is, they were really cheap. To buy, that is. Because I have spent at least ten times as much maintaining them as I did buying them nearly twenty years ago. When John Jacob Astor said: 'If you have to ask how much it costs, you can't afford it', he was talking about boats and he knew what he was talking about. At that point, I draw breath and say, not too complacently I hope (Was it imagination or did one of my offspring just say: 'Come on, get real!'?), they are both, of course, wooden boats.

I have a hunch that considerably more than nine out of ten Americans—how about 9,999 out of 10,000 as a rough approximation?—are unaware of the revival of wooden boats, particularly in the USA and Britain since the 1970s. But the revival has indeed occurred and if wooden boatpersons do not cruise around shouting 'Alleluia', that is only because they would feel conspicuous. On the other hand, since wooden boats now account for a tiny proportion of the boat population, and they would only have to shout when they met another wooden boat, it might be all right. Anyway, the triumphant progress of the wooden boat boom has been chronicled and celebrated in a superb American magazine devoted to building wooden boats, preserving wooden boats, and sailing wooden boats. Predictably—which is not a shortcoming among broadminded people—it is called *Wooden Boat*. More recently, two similar journals for hard-case wooden boat freaks, *The Boatman* and *Classic Boat*, have appeared in England where, for several years now you have been able to buy *Wooden Boat* in what are sometimes called—rather uppishly, I always think—selected outlets. That may suggest wooden boat people are elitist when they are in fact among the very nicest people you could hope to find anywhere. Which is to say everywhere, because—in my admittedly limited experience—people who care about garboards and knees and grown oak stems are much the same in Norfolk, England as in Norfolk, Virginia. And if I am to believe the message of *Wooden Boat*—which, of course, I do, implicitly—wherever wooden boats are built, sailed, and cared for there are down-to-earth, sane, enjoyable people.

That, however, is not really surprising. Wooden boats have a way of making you humble as well as hard up, although I suspect that a new wooden boat bought in England is still cheaper than in the States. That puts it, by my reckoning, on a very short and fast-shrinking list. In fact the only other things that leap to mind are cut flowers, plants from garden centres, and hand-made or—as they say in California these days—'designer' bread.

Wooden boats get under your skin. You get to love the sounds they make: wooden hulls resonate like a well-tuned 'cello; plastic hulls make empty, echoing noises. And while those who love wooden boats will ultimately admit they are faintly absurd—they rot, they leak, they crack, they get unfastened—they will also ask you what is wrong with the absurd; why the compulsion to be rational?

It may stretch things a bit, but it seems to me the wooden boat is an apt motif for our time, precisely because it represents the blend of the rational and the absurd or, if you prefer, of science and humanity, for which western civilization is frantically seeking in a post-nuclear world. A few months ago, I was greatly impressed by a book called *Cosmopolis* by Stephen Toulmin, a transplanted English academic who teaches philosophy at Northwestern University near Chicago. His essential thesis is that in the early seventeenth century, western civilization became infatuated with the science of Newton and the philosophy of Descartes and, in the process, all but severed its humanistic roots. The world of Shakespeare was thus very different from the world of Sheridan a century later. Toulmin then argues that it is only recently—since the 1960s—that one can detect in the west a partial reversion to humanism and thus towards what oriental cultures have always had and never lost.

Partial reversion does not mean replacement. It means the fusion of art and science. A few months ago, Vaclav Havel, who just last week stopped being president of Czechoslovakia, made a remarkable speech in Davos. It had a very similar theme, but a much greater sense of urgency, driven by the need—in what George Bush calls the 'New World Order'—for rapprochement between east and west.

Now it may strike some people as faintly—or even extraordinarily—ridiculous to say that the wooden boat is an apt motif for the 'New World Order'. But it certainly represents the fusion of technology and craftsmanship. Of course, there is fine craftsmanship in a well-built and well finished fibreglass (or as it is called in England, glass reinforced plastic) boat. And yes, fibreglass is derived from natural materials if one allows for the numerous industrial processes involved in the transformation of silica and crude petroleum. But the difference is that wooden boats have been around as long as boats have been around. The first boat was a hollowed log, whereas fibreglass is the quintessence of the age of reason. So it seems to me—even if I am stretching Professor Toulmin's ideas a bit, and interpreting President Havel's thoughts in a way he might disallow—that wooden boats are anchored in the philosophy of scientific humanism. The craftsmen who build and repair wooden boats today use power tools at every turn. But a lapstrake (or, in England, clinker) hull looks and is, much the same today as in the seventeenth century, just as wooden cross-country skis, laminated though they now are, can trace their origins over several centuries of Nordic craftsmanship; and yes, I do have wooden skis too.

Today, it would be an expensive proposition to build either of 'my' boats. The bigger one, a twelve-square-metre Sharpie, was built by Lester Southerland at Brancaster Staithe in 1947. Parts of her hard-chine hull have been replaced. Also the decks. And the mast tabernacle. And the spars. But, new bits and old bits, she is as sound today as she was when new although she will sit out the dance of this summer, high and dry in Rodney Crafer's field barn off the Dry Road (so called because there are no pubs) from Wells to Fakenham, more than a mile from the slipway of Wells Sailing Club.

The Sharpie is a heavy boat for her size—more than 500 lbs. in the hull alone—and a complex boat, as any gaff-rigged boat is apt to be. When my brother-in-law Gary and I bought her in 1973, *Tinqua*, named like many other Sharpies after a nineteenth century tea-clipper, had a unique wishbone tiller, itself a thing of wooden beauty, that now hangs at one end of our converted coach-house in Binham. She had no winches; the sheets came straight through the fairleads into your hands. None of the other things that have gradually since then been incorporated in Sharpies, having originated as go-fast gear in more modern boats like Fireballs and Five-O-Fives.

In England the Sharpie is and has always been a racing boat. In Holland, where there are more of them and where Sharpie sailors must be smaller—which means those I have seen cannot be typical—Sharpies are sometimes used for cruising and camping. Rather them than me; the Sharpie is not built for comfort, with a low boom and narrow wells either side of the centreplate case which, is where they sleep. Despite modernization, today's Sharpie could be described as an anachronism. Or as the nautical equivalent of a vintage car. I can see the other point of view, but I'd say the Sharpie is a truly classic boat.

It is hard to imagine, looking at the high-tech sailing machines at the Barcelona Olympics which started today, that the Sharpie was selected as the two-person centreboard class at the Melbourne Olympics in 1956. One of the British boats was from Brancaster Staithe, home of Brancaster Sailing Club and at that time one of the major Sharpie centres in Britain. Now, forty or so years later, Brancaster is again becoming a Sharpie centre, and over the years in between—even when few Sharpies were based there—it has been several times chosen as the venue for British and European Sharpie championships. The story of what happened to the Brancaster Sharpies between the Melbourne Olympics and the 1990s encapsulates forty years of sailing history in North Norfolk.

In my version of North Norfolk, the sailing scene stretches west to east from Brancaster through Burnham Overy Staithe, (known to sailors simply as Overy), Wells, Morston, and Blakeney. Only two of those places, Brancaster and Wells, have what most people would think of as sailing-clubs, with bars, toilets, and showers. There is no organized sailing at Morston, although there is a lot of unorganized sailing; and at Overy and Blakeney, there are studiously informal clubs with flag officers and secretaries but no facilities—handy pubs serve those purposes.

The Sharpie was designed in Germany in the 1930s and a handful, from such famous shipbuilders as Abeking and Rasmussen, were imported to England before the war. After the war, more came; some as war reparations, some simply carted off by the Royal Navy. By 1946 there were more than one hundred Sharpies in England, many having been given to university sailing clubs and medical schools. But within a few years, they began to turn up at, among other places, Brancaster Staithe, where they became the latest thing.

The sailing club at Brancaster was then, and is now, much better heeled than the club at Wells. And the Sharpies there were, in many cases, sailed by local watermen and crewed by their owners, few of whom lived in North Norfolk except at weekends. The Brancaster Sharpie that went to Melbourne was owned, but neither helmed, nor crewed by local sailors .

Through the 1950s the Sharpies remained fashionable, but with the advent of fibreglass hulls and new designs in the 1960s the Sharpies began to seem old fashioned. And one by one, they migrated to Wells where a sailing club had been established in the 1930s—at about the same time as at Brancaster—but whose members were fishermen and townspeople; there were few, if any, 'foreigners'. And there was certainly less money. Not nearly enough to buy new fibreglass dinghies. But enough to buy the second-hand Sharpies that came on the market as Brancaster sailors bought Fireballs, Jolly boats, and Five-O-Fives. Unfashionable but affordable; within a decade there was a fleet of more than twenty Sharpies in Wells, which had, by then become one of the few places in Britain where they remained popular. Gary and I bought *Tinqua* in 1973 for about two hundred pounds, about a fifth of the cost of a new Fireball at that time—not that I wanted one.

All old things go through a stage of being outmoded and most are then discarded. But some of them, in due course, become fashionable again. So with the Sharpies, which in recent years have been reborn at Brancaster as modish antiques. Today, there are a few at Overy, about a dozen at Brancaster, including the first new Sharpie to have been built in Britain for more than thirty years, and twice that number in Wells. With them, North Norfolk has by far the largest concentration of Sharpies in the country, the only other significant fleets being at Lymington and Langstone in Hampshire. There are many more Sharpies in Holland than in England; about as many in Germany; and a few in Australia, Brazil, and Portugal. There is no world championship, although there has been a lot of communication between Sharpie sailors in the northern and southern hemispheres. In Australia—where there are fewer inhibitions about changing things like boat designs than in England—a marine ply version of the Sharpie with a Bermudian (sloop) rig and a trapeze has become a development class. It is much faster and two of them have been built in Norfolk; both are now at Brancaster Staithe. As for the Brazilian Sharpies, I know they exist because, after a series of hilarious telephone conversations with me speaking Spanish and a succession of yacht club officers up and down the coast of Brazil speaking the Brazilian version of Portuguese, I eventually tracked down a club with a fleet of Sharpies, during visits there in the early 1980s. But I never had time to go to see them because they were too far from Rio.

Sailing on the Norfolk coast is not all about Sharpies. If you wander round the hard at Blakeney or Morston or Brancaster Staithe, you will find examples of almost every class of small boat you ever heard of and a few you have not. Most of them plastic. But go to Morston and you will find a good number of clinker-built, double-ended day boats, modelled on Cromer workboats, lying in the creek. And at Overy you will find—among more than two hundred boats—more than a dozen Twinkle Twelves which are very much at home in that hard-to-get-in-to, hard-to-get-out-of harbour that stretches in front of the black-tarred Boathouse where Peter Beck keeps both his chandlery and an eye on what is happening outside. Our own clinker boat, *Pocahontas*—an obvious name for a boat belonging to children with ties to both Virginia and Norfolk, because the Indian princess who married John Rolfe is buried at Heacham—is a Twinkle Twelve. Like *Tinqua* she's been partly rebuilt, with new decks and some new fastenings. But she's mostly original and, with the patina that only comes with well-maintained age—she has been carefully looked after by our friend, William Cracknell of Wells—none of us would dream of parting with her; a boat for ever.

We sometimes take our boats to other harbours for regattas or just for a change. But most of the time, we sail from Wells. I've never thought of sailing anywhere else. It's less picturesque than the other harbours. It has the disadvantage of a high-built quay that plays tricks with the wind. And there are fewer small boats there than elsewhere. But it is real in a way that, picture-perfect though they are, the other places aren't. Certainly that has a lot to do with the fact that Wells is still a local club and the accents in the bar are, for the most part, as local as they ever were. And there are very few members who do not sail, with the honourable exception of those who once did but are now too old to crawl or leap around a Sharpie. Few would argue that Wells Sailing Club is unpretentious but I am not sure that everyone with an opinion would say the same of the others. The absence of facilities in the large clubs at Blakeney and Overy might seem pretentious to some. So too might the barman at Brancaster; at Wells, the members take turns.

For all these differences between the sailing clubs of North Norfolk, they are trivial by comparison with the things they have in common: the same sea, the same winds, the same tide, and the same mud.

The North Sea is a notoriously unforgiving sea which does not tolerate fools at all and sometimes kills them. None of the harbours has an easy exit and entrance. With the wind off the sea, their shallow thresholds can be turbulent and dangerous. A mistake in a small boat and you may get wet—or worse. One of the reasons the Sharpie championships were held at Brancaster, when most of the Sharpies were in Wells, is that the harbour entrance is better protected; the other reasons are the larger expanse of deep water inside it, and, of course—whatever cynical comments people might make about them—the fact that the facilities are better there.

Much of the time, and at all seasons of the year, the wind blows from the west or south west. At Wells that means tacking through the quay, which is almost always a pain because the wind is fickle there; reaching down the harbour channel; and then, depending on the strength of the wind, over the bar and out to sea, or around a course protected by the offshore spit that has grown up there in the last 20 years. Even in this protected water, sailing can be treacherous. The more so when the wind comes from the north or the north west. And the more so still when it's from the north east. But by the time the northeasterlies blow strongest, most small boats have been snuggled down for the winter, well away from the playground waters of summer. The sailing season here is short: from April at the earliest and most often, May, through to September at the latest. On the Chesapeake Bay, the season starts earlier and finishes later and the best sailing is in spring and fall. A pity for Norfolk sailors that they never sail to the haunting chorus of migrating geese arriving from the Arctic. The geese are there all right—on the saltmarshes as on the Chesapeake—but by October the Norfolk air is much colder and the days are much shorter. After all, the Chesapeake is on the same latitude as Madrid and the British Isles would be uninhabitable but for the Gulf Stream.

When I tell friends in America that we can't sail just when we want to in Norfolk because of the tidal range, most of them are surprised. Particularly Chesapeake sailors, accustomed to a range of two feet or less, although those who sail in New England know more about it and those who sail in the Pacific Northwest have a story all their own. Norfolk is different because God pulls the plug out twice a day. And all that remains is mud.

Between them—though they were writing about Suffolk which, whatever anyone may tell you, is not like North Norfolk (it is like Suffolk)—Arthur Ransome, storyteller and spellbinder extraordinaire, and Maurice Griffiths, master chronicler of east coast yachting, have sung the praise of east coast mud in what seems to me a definitive fashion. Every year, I remind myself that in the spring I will make some splatchers, just like the boy in Ransome's *Secret Water* who used to walk on mud which is constitutionally like Norfolk mud even if it has the misfortune to be in Suffolk, I even thought of getting some snowshoes from L.L. Bean; after all, the principle is similar. And every year I say, next year.

There was a time, when Carey and Caitlin were much younger than they are now, when it seems—in retrospect—that they were always covered in mud: Wells mud, Overy mud, Morston mud, Brancaster mud. I cannot tell the difference and I do not believe the story that local fishermen could tell where they were in a coastal fog on the North Norfolk coast by the consistency of the mud. However, I do believe the story that their Dorset counterparts know where they are on the Chesil Bank because the pebbles are larger at Portland than near Abbotsbury—or is it the other way round?

Keelboats visiting these waters do so at their peril unless they have arranged to moor against the quay in Wells. Elsewhere, the sailor who comes in on an evening tide is likely to wake up on the cabin sole when the ebb has left his boat lying on its side surrounded by sand, or possibly by mud. That is only an inconvenience. The real fun starts when the next tide slops in over the coaming and fills the boat with water. Bilge keels make enormously good sense here. I have never been able to understand why people claim that bilge keels go better to windward than full keels or centreboarders. If they do, why aren't ocean racers made that way? No, they are a perfect example of environmental adaptation for places like North Norfolk, where your boat must regularly stand on the bottom without damaging either itself or its contents. At low tide, walk around the temporarily stranded yachts high and dry on their moorings at Brancaster or Wells and you'll find that all but a few have twin bilges. Those that do not, have centreboards, and with them the unique disadvantages of having a hole in the bottom that, sooner or later and probably both, will leak and keep leaking, and of having a knee-smashing obstacle in the middle of the cabin floor.

So sailing in North Norfolk may have been more to do with boating around in muck than mucking about (yes, I know he said 'messing" but I am using poetic licence) in boats. Somehow, though, being governed by the tides adds to the adventure. It is a reminder that where the North Sea is concerned, you can't do what you like, because the eternal backing and filling of the tides have absolute dominion. And it means that another world—the low-tide world of mud, and gillycrabs, and sandpipers, and the sucking noises made by the last remnants of the water that came in with the last tide—is there to be explored. It is a different world. And one of the most magical things about the coast of the Magic Kingdom is that, with meticulous regularity, it changes its face twice a day. And he or she who knows not both, knows not the Magic Kingdom.

27 July

This morning I woke at five something and went back to sleep. And woke again when the sun shone directly in my face. Now, since our bedroom window faces north across the grounds of Binham Priory, that cannot be true. But I am certainly awake and I am back at my table, writing.

I have often written in the early morning. But not here. Every so often, when I want to get some uninterrupted time before people start wanting to talk to me, I get up around five and I am at my desk by six thirty. I am always astonished to see how many other people are on the roads into downtown Washington at that hour. Do the same people do it every day? Or is there a sort of rota so that today it is their turn, just as it is mine, to go to the office extra early?

Early mornings have always been special to me. It's partly the new beginning, the promise of birth, the clean slate. Especially when the morning is misty and the new day emerges as a faint shape in the haze. It's partly because it sounds different. Although nature gets up early the world over, the birds and the insects of the tropics are quite unlike those of Norfolk. Even Washington is different and that's not tropical. There, in the spring and summer, when the air temperature is not so cold that we need heating and not so warm that we need air conditioning, we hear cicadas and mocking-birds. Here, my favourite morning sounds come from sheep in the middle distance. Not in the field across the lane which, when we are here in summer, is always shared, on a dayshift–nightshift basis, by a milking herd and a pair of horses. But up on the fields that slope gently towards Cockthorpe so their bleating sounds carry across the valley of the little River Stiffkey all the way to our window. On the Chesapeake Bay, my favourite sound, which is perhaps my favourite sound in all the world, is that of geese flying in ragged V-formations to their feeding grounds in the rivers that feed it.

And it's partly also because it feels different. When we first had our place in Binham, I often (which is to say more than twice) got up really early—and in July that means well before five o'clock to go for dawn walks across the country that lies between Binham and the landward edge of the marshes. Or to take Carey and Caitlin to watch rabbits, which were much less numerous then than now, doing their morning exercises among the Corsican pines behind the beach at Wells. Or to go cockling at Stiffkey, because I did not then know that the famous Stewkey Blues had long since disappeared, and fill my basket with cockles, and come home in triumph with the catch of the day although I was vaguely aware that cockles are not usually thought of as sporting fish. The real problem, however, was that nobody wanted to prepare them—which involves an awful lot of fuss and bother for a trifling yield of tough, rubbery, gristly, shellfish. We tried making cockle pie a few times from a recipe donated to a good-cause cookbook by a certain Major Hubert Blount of Cley; with a name like that how could one go wrong? And for a summer or two we were known—a bit derisively I think—as the cockle-pie people by some of our friends who live here all the time, who would not be seen dead in the act of grubbing around in the sand and mud for cockles, or of making a cockle pie.

For some reason, the urge to cockle has left me, and my cockle rake is hanging, forlorn and rusting, in the hall. Perhaps it was my discovery, on Menemsha Pond on Martha's Vineyard—where you need a town licence to go after them—of the really big clams, four or five inches across and each with as much meat as half a bucket of cockles, that are known as quahogs in New England and as cherrystones elsewhere on the Atlantic seaboard, that put me off cockles for good. Anyway, I gather the cockles are getting scarcer. Which means I can have the best of both worlds. I can leave other people to do the digging and pretend I am doing my bit for conservation.

The Bricked Up Window

I'd better start by saying I have not been to an Anglican church service —except at the end of summer terms when Carey and Caitlin were at Rugby—for more than thirty years. And perhaps I should add that I am a bad Quaker—not having been to a Meeting for Worship for about two years.

I have not been to the Meeting House in Wells—where Glynis and I exchanged promises in the do-it-yourself tradition of Quaker marriage in 1964, and where I have been a member for thirty years—because it would clash with sailing, which, as the tide turns, is a Sunday morning matter every other week. And I have not been to the Meeting House at Bethesda, Maryland, for reasons that have nothing to do with North Norfolk, and since I can decide what goes in here and what does not, I offer no further explanation. Suffice it to say—what an awful phrase, but it will do—that I find plenty of other things to do at my house in McLean on Sunday mornings. (Note: 10.56 am, Sunday, 6 September, 1992: Such as transcribing my handwritten text on a portable computer.)

Oddly, though, when we have been to the Vineyard in summer we have always been to Meeting for Worship on Sunday mornings. Not, at least in my case, because of piety. Nor because Meeting for Worship takes place in the tiniest chapel you've ever seen, which was built in the sixteenth century wilderness for the mission to the Algonquin tribe that then inhabited the Vineyard. Some wilderness. Or because it is comfortable sitting on the narrowest pews you've ever sat on, so that you spend a lot of time wondering whether the Algonquins had deformed bottoms or whether the missionaries thought the way to God was through anal cramp. Or because the chapel is old, because if that were the motive, why don't I walk across the lane to the Priory church which had its nine-hundredth birthday last year?

No, I think the main reason is that, on the Vineyard, going to Quaker Meeting is an opportunity to meet people who live there all the time. All of them are immigrants who have settled there in mid-career or on retirement, but they are part of the select nine thousand who live there all year round and see the population swell fivefold between June and September. Going to church—or to Meeting—to meet people is, I suspect, consistent with the concept of the church as the centre of the community.

In North Norfolk, it was not so long ago that the magnificent churches of the Anglican tradition—many of which were, of course, there long before there was an Anglican tradition—were indeed the centres of the communities around them. In the gently undulating terrain of the Magic Kingdom, their towers and steeples and spires stand out in the man-made landscape (perhaps we should call it the 'manscape'; after all, garden designers in the States now refer routinely to things like pergolas, arbours and fountains as elements of the 'hardscape'), bearing witness to the continuity of rural life that until recently revolved around them.

For reasons that had much more to do with my then girlfriend—who sang in the choir—than with God, there was a period of a few years while I was at school in Willesden, when I regularly attended Anglican services. I even got so involved that I would read the lessons in a purple cassock and white gown. And in the summer before my final year, I wrote a long essay for a competition, on the topic of 'The future of the Church of England'. I remember finishing it by quoting a then bishop, whose name I do not remember, who had written: 'The Church of England in its present state, no power on earth can save', which summarized my rather confused conclusions better than I could summarize them myself. Although the judges were not impressed by my work —not enough, anyway, to award me a prize —it seems to me that both of us (the nameless bishop and myself) were on to something. The Anglican community has continued to shrink and the average age of the population—and thus one might think the numbers of those who are not too busy with work and family to go to church—has continued to rise. And there are fewer and fewer parish priests and those there are must cover a larger number of village churches, with the result that there are fewer and fewer regular services in each of them.

For some reason—it is not religious—I am, from time to time, tempted to go to an Anglican service. Not to meet people. I already know them because they are my neighbours here in Binham. But to hear the glorious and ethereal sound of a church or cathedral choir. One of the things I liked best about visiting Rugby was the sound of end-of-term services, when young voices, rough at the edges but lusty and profoundly moving, brought back memories of ends of terms at my grammar school in London. There, we sang:

Lord dismiss us with thy blessing
All who here shall meet no more...

And at Rugby they sang:

Lord be with us 'till we meet again...

But the sentiment was the same, although the chapel of Rugby School provides a rather different atmosphere from the school hall cum gymnasium at my school.

I hesitate to go, however, because I wonder whether that is a sound reason for going to the Priory Church of St Mary's, or to Norwich Cathedral where I presume the choral music would be a lot better—and which is not so far away I could not get there if I made an effort. A choral service is not, after all, a free concert for the heathen. Or is it?

The Anglican churches that decorate North Norfolk are among its chief glories. Some are older than the priory church at Binham. The nearest village going west, Warham, has two churches; another St Mary's and All Saints'. They stand at either end of the village which today has a population of fewer than three hundred, memorials to the time when this community was much larger and there were two parishes. They must, however, have been cheek by jowl because the churches are only half a mile apart. St Mary's is now locked most of the time because vandalism has washed up here too and the casual visitor is denied access to the magnificent high-backed sixteenth-century pews. Its churchyard contains the recent grave of Sir Roy Harrod, whose gravestone is inscribed: 'Knight, Economist'. I wondered, until recently, why the former Oxford professor, who with Evsey Domar—whom I remember meeting a long time ago in Colombia—created a famous model of economic growth, was buried in Warham. And then someone told me he had Norfolk origins and that his wife was from the Turner family which, historically, was *the* Warham family to come from. It is a quietly beautiful place and I should think it is just about the perfect place to be buried; if, that is, you are buried at all.

The two largest churches in my North Norfolk are at Blakeney and Cley. Any guidebook will tell you that both of them reflect the prosperity of those villages at the time—in both cases the fifteenth century—they were built. Prosperity came not from the sea but from access to the sea. The quay at Blakeney—which is still intact—once berthed half a dozen trading vessels at a time, with others waiting in Blakeney Pit for their turns to deliver building materials and household goods and to carry away wool from the vast sheep-run of the hinterland. The old quay at Cley is, however, long since gone; the wall that backs the reedy marsh below Cley mill is a much later structure. If you want to know where the quay was when Cley, like Blakeney, was a busy port, you must go nearly a mile inland towards the church of St Margaret's, whose noble proportions and large size speak to the wealth of the medieval port. Whereas Blakeney's church—dedicated like that of Wells to St Nicholas, the patron of seafarers—was deliberately sited on the highest available ground, a rise of nearly two hundred feet, as a landmark for sailors; Cley Church is until you get close to it low and inconspicuous.

If it is easier to reconstruct the ancient relationship between church and quay at Blakeney than at Cley, try Wiveton for size. A mile farther inland, up the valley of the River Glaven—which, in local terms, would be puny were it not for the even punier River Stiffkey that, even in only moderately dry summers, goes out of business entirely and in other places would not be called a river at all—Wiveton does not look like a former port. But it was, because until certain parts of the North Norfolk coast were reconfigured for ever by drainage projects that began in the sixteenth century, Wiveton sat beside a tidal inlet. It too was a wool port although the relatively smaller size of its church (another St Mary's; she was obviously a popular lady around here in the Middle Ages) suggests it was less prosperous than Blakeney and Cley. The church of St Nicholas at Wells is less interesting than most because it is a nineteenth-century replacement for a medieval structure destroyed by fire in 1879 when it was struck by lightning.

The seven 'Burnhams by the sea' were originally defined by their churches. The largest of them, Burnham Market, has two churches because it was once, more plausibly than Warham, two villages: Burnham Westgate and Burnham Sutton, which merged in the eighteenth century. The most interesting Burnham churches, however, are at Overy Town, Burnham Norton, and Burnham Thorpe.

The fifteenth century tower on the church of the tiny village of Overy Town—a misnomer of current reality if there ever was one—sits quaintly in the centre of the building, which is not very large, and stands on a slight rise on the road to Wells. The marsh-hugging village of Burnham Norton is separated from its church by more than a mile and is actually closer to Burnham Market, yet it was a long time before I thought of this as more than a curiosity and asked why. The answer, it turned out, was that the original settlement was abandoned when the Black Death hit it in the fourteenth century, and the village was re-established near the marshes. The church, however, stayed put, and its distance from the new village must have called for an extra measure of piety on Sunday mornings. It was presumably forthcoming, for the church was as much used as any other parish church until the old social and religious order began to decompose after the First World War.

By far the most visited of the Burnham churches is yet another St Mary's, at Burnham Thorpe, where Horatio Nelson's father, Edmund, was rector for more than three decades that spanned the eighteenth and nineteenth centuries. North Norfolk's favourite son was born there, spent much of his childhood there, and lived there again, unhappily, as a captain on half-pay before the war with France gave him the opportunity to become famous. The rectory was pulled down in the nineteenth century with a typical Victorian innocence of fortunes to be made from things of the past.

All the tourist finds today is an engraved plate on what is thought—presumably accurately—to be the site. The church, however, is crammed with Nelson memorabilia. If that does not suffice, Les Winter, the landlord of 'The Lord Nelson' has a special room where he keeps his Nelson stuff and if he likes you he'll let you see it and invite you to buy a tee-shirt which bears the inevitable legend.

My own favourite churches in the Magic Kingdom—if, as a member of the Great Unwashed, I am entitled to favourites—are the church of St Andrew's at Little Snoring and, perhaps because I live so close to it (although, since it gets so many visitors, a lot of other people must think it is special too), the priory church of St Mary's on the other side of the lane from our house here in Binham.

People elsewhere always think Little Snoring is a made-up name, of the same genre as Much Binding in the Marsh, which I dimly recall as a radio-place when I was a small child. It has a superb round tower, possibly though not certainly of Saxon origin, and whenever I pass it—and it's the sort of place I try to pass, even if it's not on the way to where I'm going—I shiver slightly with delight that whatever their other deficiencies, the church builders who began this building in the twelfth century had a rare instinct for what people like me would want to see eight centuries later. Even though Professor Pevsner describes Little Snoring church as 'rough' and 'crude' in parts, the result, to my way of thinking, is magnificent.

The priory church at Binham is a remnant. Originally, the nave was twice as long as it is now, which is to say the altar (the earlier site of which is clearly marked) was way beyond the present east end, which was constructed after Henry VIII threw the last remaining monks out of the priory in the sixteenth century. The nave was also much wider at that time because there were side chapels prior to dissolution. Henry does not, however, deserve all the credit for creating the exquisitely beautiful ruins that now surround the priory church. Two things about it particularly delight me. One is the great west window. It is the first thing you see when you come through what is left of the arched gatehouse from the road and it was bricked up in 1809 after the window had fallen into disrepair. And it has since become so famous, partly through the efforts of John Sell Cotman and other painters of the Norwich School in the nineteenth century and many other artists between then and now, that there would surely be a huge commotion if anybody thought it would be nice to improve it by replacing the glass; a bricked up window it is likely to remain. The other thing that delights me is the intimate juxtaposition of churchyard and farmyard which accounts for the many photographs of ancient gravestones set against a background of barns and silos. I hesitate to think that anything, anywhere is perfect because it seems to me, as to the rug-makers of ancient Persia, that perfection is unattainable, or as Keats put it:

A man's reach should exceed his grasp
Or what's a Heaven for?

But Binham, as the great state of West Virginia proclaims itself to be on its automobile licence tags, seems to me 'Almost heaven'. And there was I thinking I don't believe in anything any more. Perhaps I do, after all.

What amazes me most about these churches, particularly those at Blakeney and Cley, is that until this century they stood in such dramatic contrast to the homes of their parishioners. But not to the homes of those charged with their spiritual care. North Norfolk, like the rest of England, is now full of old rectories (not many old vicarages) which contrast strangely with the decidedly modest new rectories where the few remaining rectors live. Since, however, the churches are all very much older than the old rectories, the clergy obviously lived somewhere else before the eighteenth century when the Church Commissioners, or their predecessors, started the building boom that has given us so many old rectories in the Georgian style. The Old Rectory at Wells where our friends, Dick and Sheila Griffiths-Jones, now live is a fine example of the type. Just as the modern house on the other side of their property line is a good example of where the rectors live now.

I contend that the eighteenth and nineteenth centuries, and the first half of this one, were an aberration and that historically the Church of England was not in the perpetual care of priests who lived relatively high on the hog. What were the older rectories like, such as the one in Burnham Thorpe where Nelson grew up? There are some clues in the Old Rectory at East Barsham, which for the last twenty-six years has rejoiced in the delightful name of Toad Hall. Until its then new owners gave it that name, the property had always—that is, as far as there are records to show—been owned by the Church and indeed the parish church occupies what might be thought of as the south-east corner of the front garden.

The rectory was actually built in four phases, the sixteenth century core of the existing building being the first. The original house was not insubstantial. It was on three floors with only two rooms on each level, suggesting that, although the pre-eighteenth century parsons lived comfortably, their homes were modest by comparison with those of their successors. The three subsequent phases, the last a Victorian splurge, produced the house of eleven bedrooms, not counting those in the domestic wing (where there were four more), and a comprehensive range of outbuildings, including coach-house and brew-house. East Barsham Old Rectory was not exceptionally large or unusually splendid. In fact it lacks much of the elegance of other rectories that were built all of a piece, with a coherent design. Having grown, organically as it were, there are few gracious rooms, the best ones in terms of proportion, being those added last.

If indeed country parsons lived well but not extremely well before the eighteenth century, there can be no doubt that for about two hundred years thereafter the Anglican clergy lived in a style that was high by our own standards, and must have been grotesque by those of the time. Not far away, just off the Fakenham–Norwich road, is the village of Weston Longville where James Woodforde was parson for sixty years that spanned the end of the century and the start of the next one. His record of daily life, preserved and published as *The Diary of a Country Parson* , was one of the surprise hits of the 1980s and I found it, as I tend to find all such accounts, fascinating reading. The interesting question is, why is it fascinating?

On one level it is a monument to gluttony. How could Parson Woodforde and his friends have eaten so much? For example, on 28 January 1780 he wrote:

> We had, for dinner, a Calf's Head, boiled Fowl and Tongue, a Saddle of Mutton roasted on the Side Table, and a fine Swan roasted with Currant Jelly for the First Course. The Second Course a couple of Wild Fowl called Dun Fowls, Larks, Blamange, Tarts etc. and a good Dessert of Fruit after, amongst which was a Damson Cheese.

To be sure this was a special occasion, but whenever I read bits of it—it is the sort of stuff you can read and re-read—I have a mental image of grossly overweight men and women who probably did not walk thirty yards a day, let alone the thirty miles that might have worked up such enormous appetites, spending at least half their waking hours eating and drinking and staggering away from the table afterwards. Did they only take small helpings? Somehow I doubt it. This was after all a long time before nouvelle cuisine had taught us the virtues of arranging small quantities of food in enticing ways, so that each course is insubstantial. And Woodforde never mentions vegetables. But this was Norfolk and I am unable to imagine the Woodforde table did not contain mountains of potatoes, mounds of carrots, and heaps of peas as well as the results of busy mornings blasting at everything that moved in the fields and hedgerows.

On another level—and, I think, a more relevant one—the

Woodforde diaries are fascinating precisely because they deal with the (then) ordinary. They lift the veil that protects the domestic world of rural Norfolk two centuries ago, and give the reader an idea of what life was like, not only for the parson in his comfortable rectory but also—because he was a good and, I suspect, innocent observer—for those who worked in and supported agriculture just before the Agricultural Revolution began only a few miles away at Holkham and Raynham.

Today, the Anglican parishes of North Norfolk all seem to be combined: Binham with Hindringham and Langham; Wells with Warham and Wighton and so on. The question must arise, what will happen to the churches when the few who now worship in them die off? Although I have made my own lack of religious allegiance clear, I think it would be a national, even an international, tragedy if even one of them fell down for want of money to look after it. I have no idea how much wealth the Church of England still has. But if it cannot maintain them, the rest of us—Godless and Godfearing (what a word!)—will have to do so. No part of North Norfolk's manscape is more worth preserving.

It is a matter of record that the Church of England—traditionally the Tory Party at prayer—has usually protected the status quo; radical bishops, priests and deacons are inventions of the twentieth century. But in North Norfolk there was an intimate connexion between the development of the Nonconformist churches, particularly the Methodist Church, and radical politics.

Unlike the Anglican churches—I suppose one could say the churches of England—none of which in North Norfolk has been deconsecrated, many former Nonconformist churches have become other things; where pastors and lay preachers once put the fear of God into their audiences there are now shops, galleries, and private homes. From an architectural point of view, it seems to me that the only question that arises is whether they should have been pulled down instead and the land rather than the fabric used for some other purpose. They are, almost uniformly, ugly; their dark red brick reminds me of grimy industrial buildings in the north of England.

But from the viewpoint of social history the austere Nonconformist chapels are reminders of a time, not so long ago, when their equally austere congregations found a seamless continuity between a weekday world of political confrontation and economic survival and a Sunday world of religious inspiration. The growth of the Labour Party and of the Agricultural Workers' Union in North Norfolk and the spectacular success of the Methodist and (to a lesser extent) Congregational churches in the Magic Kingdom were tightly interwoven in the ebbing years of the nineteenth century and the early years of the twentieth.

It was Nonconformism that sent Lord Noel Buxton, first as a Liberal, then as a Socialist, to the House of Commons. He was succeeded by Edwin Gooch, who carried his Dickensian name to success in every national election ballot from 1945 to 1963. He was still—by a year or so—the MP for North Norfolk when I first came here. The constituency naturally included (and still includes) a much larger area than the Magic Kingdom and at that it time had been continuously held by the Labour Party for more than forty years. Superficially it was hard to see why. Few people worked on the land although more did then than now. The rectors still lived in their rectories. The Earl of Leicester lived in Holkham Hall. The constituency—both the Magic Kingdom part and the other parts—was superficially very much like dozens of other constituencies up and down England that returned Conservative members and had done so, in most cases for decades. Why was North Norfolk (formally known, I suppose, as Norfolk, North) different?

The answer was that the Labour Party here was deeply rooted in the Agricultural Workers' Union, which in turn was deeply rooted in the Nonconformist churches. In the early 1960s, that tradition was still alive. Its grasp on reality was of course slipping as mechanization moved in on the few remaining agricultural processes still performed by hand and the agricultural workforce diminished yet further, having shrunk dramatically between the wars and more dramatically after 1945. But the electorate clung, for a few more years, to the radical tradition and, to a large extent, voted for Edwin Gooch rather than what he stood for.

With Gooch's retirement political criteria rather than sentiment ascended, and from tentative beginnings in the 1960s when North Norfolk remained—incongruously to those who did not understand—a marginal seat, it has since become a safe Conservative haven and seems likely to stay that way indefinitely. The population has changed. Many former tenants of the council houses built before and after the war in every village in the Magic Kingdom have become property-owning democrats as the local authorities that have taken care of the detailed political affairs of the Magic Kingdom have sold them off to tenants. The new housing and the farm buildings that have been converted to residential use are occupied either by people who can afford second homes or have come from elsewhere to retire, most of whom, it seems, have voted Conservative as long as they can remember.

The Quaker Meeting House at Wells is the only one in the Magic Kingdom and it played a unique part in the local union between religion and radical politics. In 1925, when agriculture still accounted—directly or indirectly—for most of the local economy and for a larger share of employment, a young Methodist and his wife, Sam and Annie Peel, became wardens of Wells Meeting. Few Quaker Meetings have wardens because a basic tenet of the Society of Friends is that ministers are both superfluous and inappropriate. But then Wells Meeting has always been rather unusual; there had been wardens before the Peels and there have been others since.

The job of a warden has never been equivalent to that of a minister. In a conventional Friends' Meeting there are no sermons. The Meeting for Worship is not led by anyone in particular, although one or two 'weighty Friends' serve as 'elders' and open and close the Meeting (and also provide discipline if it is needed). The Meeting, which usually lasts about an hour, may contain unbroken silence. Or the silence may be broken by those—anyone in the room—who are moved to speak. There is no music unless somebody is moved to sing; certainly no hymns. In most meeting houses around the world, the benches—not pews —are arranged in a square, the 'elders' sitting side by side on one of the front ones, known as the 'facing bench'. Meeting houses are deliberately austere; there is no decoration, save perhaps a small bowl of fresh flowers on a central table.

All of which makes it odd that Wells Meeting House became known for some three decades as 'Sam Peel's Chapel'. None of those who now make up Wells Meeting was there at that time. And little by little the physical evidence has been removed. But in 1962, when I first went there, having never been inside a meeting house before, it looked quite unlike anything I have seen since then on three continents. There was a platform or dais, a full three feet above the floor. There were rows of chairs, not benches, facing it. There was a pedal organ to one side. And there were framed homilies, among them, I remember, something called 'The Good Indian's Prayer' that had lines like the ones about having:

The courage to change the things I can change
And to endure the things l cannot change,
And the wisdom to know the difference

Things like that have since become very popular items in gift shops and I have sometimes seen them hanging in people's offices. There is in my view nothing wrong with them, except that they tend to oversimplify. They were, however, like the platform and the pedal organ, a bit incongruous in a Friends' meeting house. But then, Sam put them there. Why would he have done that?

I met Sam only once, when I was in my second year at University College and Sam was a physical shadow, living quietly with his married daughter on Mill Road in Wells. By then, not only in the Magic Kingdom but in the county of Norfolk, Sam was a living legend and I remember wishing I had a tape recorder with me because I realized I was hearing history not from a historian but from a history-maker. For Sam Peel there was a natural and unbreakable connexion between Nonconformity and Socialism. In the 1920s, when Sam first arrived in Wells, this now tranquil landscape was in turmoil. The Agricultural Workers' Union, its membership swollen by farm workers who had survived the war, was fighting both the farmers—owners and tenants alike—who employed its members and a rival union. Disputes were fierce. Sam was a powerful orator and he spoke with passionate belief about the cause of the AWU. He spoke at political gatherings. He spoke at union meetings. And he spoke at the Meeting House, which little by little was transformed from a Friends' meeting to a *sui generis* congregation where orators orated, hymns were sung, and an innocent Quaker visiting from somewhere else must have thought he had come to the wrong address.

Those who opposed Sam also feared him, and more than one effort was made to shut him up. On one occasion only a timely warning of an ambush down the road on which he was driving back to Wells averted what could have been the most calamitous encounter of all. Sam became well known and, before long, politically successful, and his name is now honoured in the Alderman Peel High School in Wells. Today, when there are too few agricultural workers to make up a strong local chapter of the AWU, it is hard to envisage the Magic Kingdom as the scene of bitter social conflict. But it happened. And as one measures historical time, it happened only yesterday.

As though the conditions of agricultural labourers were not cause enough, Sam Peel also took on another enemy. It came in bottles. Having decided for his own reasons that alcohol was the devil's brew, he also decided the devil should be checked. When Sam came to Wells, there were more than fifty pubs in a town of fewer than three thousand people, not counting the visiting mariners whose vessels—many of them still under sail and thus requiring relatively large crews—came and went, in much larger numbers than now to and from Wells quay. Sam decided the town should be cleaned up. So he began what is best described as a crusade to liberate the people of Wells, and its visiting sailors, from the evils of the bottle. Not surprisingly, this created even more fuss than his promotion of the AWU and there were many, brewers and regulars alike, who violently opposed him.

Sam was nonetheless remarkably successful, if success is measured in the number of pub closings between the 1920s and the outbreak of war. I suspect—just a professional bias perhaps—that economics had something to do with it too, but the results are beyond dispute. When Sam started his charge there were more than fifty; by 1960 more than thirty Wells pubs had closed. Since then, without a campaign of any kind against them, the decline has continued. In my memory, the 'Eight Ringers' on Church Plain, the 'Vine' not far away up the High Street, the 'Ship' on the corner of the quay where Freeman Street begins, the 'Prince of Wales' at the top of Staithe Street, and the 'Park Tavern' at the western end of town, all closed in the 1960s and 1970s; and two years ago the last unmodernized pub, the 'Shipwrights Arms' served its last pint and is now falling into ruin on the best of all possible sites at the bottom of Jolly Sailors Yard.

Today, near Sculthorpe, I passed a former Primitive Methodist chapel. Only the front wall is being preserved in what is otherwise a new building. Not a bad compromise, I suppose. But that dark red brick really is ugly. The Salvation Army developed its own kind of music because, they said, the devil should not have all the best tunes. The Nonconformists obviously did not feel the same way about the Church of England and its buildings, because they made no effort to compete with its architecture, which without exception—and I am, of course, speaking of the Magic Kingdom, not in general, although it may be generally true too—has graceful lines, strength of purpose and hand-hewn artistry that defies imitation. Whether or not the institution that built them is now moribund—as an objective observer might tell you it is—I cannot imagine what the Magic Kingdom would be like if they were not here. If they are no longer the anchors of society, they are still the anchors of the landscape. Not simply because they are old; but because they are magnificent; because they are permanent; and because they encapsulate, give or take a few years, a millennium of English history. We could not be without them.

28 July

It happened again. When I looked at my watch it was 5.52 and the sun ***was*** *shining in my face. So I went to the window and looked across the field to the church, surrounded by the ruins of the priory, just to make sure it hadn't moved in the night. Then I got the answer. My house* ***does*** *face north. But somehow, in nearly twenty years, I hadn't noticed the church is not perpendicular to my wall; it is in fact at 45 degrees to it. That is because, as churches do everywhere I suppose, it points east. I felt a bit silly. Not for the first time. There was, for example, the time in Colorado, near the north rim of the Grand Canyon, when I unlocked the flap on the side of our Motor Home and wondered, for at least a minute, why the gasoline was bubbling and spurting, before I realized I was filling the water tank by mistake. That was a lot worse, come to think of it. After all there were no consequences to realizing I had got my compass bearings mixed up. Anyway, I quickly realized—was I on the ball or what!—that it had never happened before because, until this week, I had never slept on the side of the room where the sun would slant across our bedroom and into my sleeping face. Mystery solved.*

I am actually finding that all this self-imposed freedom to write about whatever I feel is relevant is hard to get used to. Usually I limit myself to clarifying the facts, identifying the issues, rigorously analysing them, and presenting reasoned and dispassionate arguments for one sort of action or another. Here the only real constraint—that I am aware of—is my own sense of what fits and what does not.

Accordingly—a useful word that I find I use much more often than 'therefore' or 'thus'—I can decide that what I want to write about today is ... architecture. No, that was in the last section. How about more on boats? And cruising. And some contrasts with cruising on the Chesapeake Bay?

Short Voyages

One of the great things about sailing on the Chesapeake Bay is that it is very easy to weigh anchor in one harbour and drop it in another. There are, quite literally, thousands of anchorages around the Bay and the distances between them are short. The quality of this experience has little to do with the length or character of the voyage. True, you tend to remember best the short voyages made with a steady breeze on the beam, a moderate swell throwing spray from the bow, a brilliant sky, clotted clouds with wombs of white sunlight, and an air temperature warm enough to be comfortable but not hot enough to threaten sunstroke. In retrospect, of course, they are all like that.

Except those when the sky was a sullen dark grey, and it rained so hard you had to keep asking someone to wipe the water off your glasses, and you wondered what in hell you were doing there. Were we having fun yet? In retrospect they were all like that too.

Except those when the sun made every surface hot to touch, reminding you it was just dumb to forget your floppy hat yet again. The surface of the Bay was what Chesapeake waterman call slick ca'am, and the mainsail slatted uselessly from port to starboard and back again until, cursing, you hit the black rubber button and turned the key to start the diesel and spent the rest of the day pretending you were a powerboat. In retrospect none of them was like that.

Despite my yearnings for and deep fascination with sailboats of most shapes and sizes (even those made of what woodenboatpersons call 'the other stuff'), I must confess that for me the best bit of every voyage begins with what would be called—if one had crossed an ocean or even a sea—a landfall. But on the Chesapeake Bay, where you are never out of sight of land, it would be more than a bit silly to talk about 'landfalls'. Instead you go through the ritual of saying, 'Oh my God, I think that's actually the right buoy (Americans call them 'boo-ees' by the way). How about that?' And you are mercifully delivered to the entrance of the creek where you have decided to spend the night.

The next bit can be disconcerting. One of the other Great Things about the Great Bay is that it is virtually rockless. So running aground is rarely a sinking matter. The downside is that the tidal range is so small that even if you wait until the next tide, if you are hard on (as they say), you are unlikely to get off unaided. On the other hand, the Bay has such an enormous population of boats that there's always somebody about to pull you off. Well, almost always. Everybody runs aground. But hardly anybody runs aground all the time. In fact, you are usually lucky, and you don't get stuck as you inch ahead at the slowest possible speed that prevents the engine from stalling. Amazingly often—but when you consider the Bay has an eight-thousand-mile shoreline, perhaps it isn't all that amazing—you'll find yourself in a sheltered, leafy anchorage which, depending on the time of day and the time of year, may also be empty. Then you find exactly the right place to drop the anchor, go backwards a bit to make sure it's dug in, and then, all being well, there is a hushful silence when the engine is cut. It doesn't last long—the silence, that is—because there are things to do. But that moment of arrival, 'finished with engines; aye aye, sir', is always for me a moment of slight triumph. That may well be the measure of me as a sailor; and if so I don't give a damn.

The most important thing to be done is called sundowning. This means everybody gets to have a nice long drink. And then another. And maybe, after that, yet another; it's not as though anybody had to drive home. There is a naval tradition of waiting for sundowners until the sun is over the proverbial yardarm. That's not really applicable on a thirty-foot yacht (actually the American term 'sailboat' is simpler, just like the 'cottages' they built in Newport in the last century).

Yardarms are not applicable on thirty footers because thirty footers do not have yardarms. I dare say you could have a yardarm on a boat that size—along with ratlines and lots of baggywrinkle—as long as you didn't mind looking ridiculous. It seems to me the simpler solution is to forget about yardarms altogether and just use good judgement about when sundowner time begins. Certainly you don't have to wait until the sun is really down; in the middle of the year you could be suffering from dehydration by then.

After the sundowners comes the ceremony of Lighting the Stove. In my (admittedly limited) experience, ships' stoves are inhabited by evil spirits. Even those on US-built boats, which, by and large, make as many concessions to comfort as those built in the UK make to sailing ability. Nearly always, it starts. When it doesn't, forget about ordering in a pizza; they won't deliver to boats unless the boat is tied to something solid, like a dock. Branches of overhanging trees don't qualify. Then comes cooking, about which the least said, in my view, the better. Especially if we've forgotten the can-opener again.

The best is still to come. You haven't tried going to bed yet. No problem in the pointy berths in the bow; legs actually do taper quite nicely, particularly small legs. But the cabin berths are another matter. They always have cushions on them so you have somewhere to sit when you're eating breakfast and dinner. Usually, the berth cushions on American boats are covered in a nubbly sort of tweed material in tastefully co-ordinated colours; the Americans call them 'designer colours'.

The point at issue though is not really their colour. It is the fact that the back cushions have to be put away so you can lie down. The back ones because, if you don't remove them, you have a narrow bench about twelve inches wide to sleep on. And unless I am mistaken, that is simply not enough. The question is: where do you put them at night?

I think berth cushions that don't belong on the berth when you actually want to use it as a berth have something in common with 'space saver' spare tyres. They're the ones that sit harmlessly in the boot or the trunk—I forget which is which—of your car in a very small space until you actually need to use them. You remove the punctured tyre and replace it with the spare, which looks as if it's made of solid rubber and has labels on it that say you should not drive at more than twenty-five miles an hour. Then, the question: where do you put the punctured one? It certainly won't fit in the space designed for the spare. And, as luck would have it, the car is stuffed to the gills with holiday luggage and small children. Interesting problem. Someone should offer a prize for the most creative answer to the question that immediately preoccupies you: what is the most hideous punishment that could be measured out to the inventor of the space saver spare?

In due course, you solve the problem (the berth cushion problem, that is). You put them on the floor. Or you throw them overboard (not a good idea; you'll need them at breakfast) and settle down for the night. In the morning, you may be woken by the haunting honking of geese as they look for somewhere to feed. Or by the sailor who came in to the anchorage well after dark last night—long after sensible sailors had been anchored for hours—and spent half an hour crashing about before he settled down. This morning, he has woken up to find that a dinghy is not like a horse, which when you put its reins over a rail stays put; you have to tie it to the boat. Otherwise it floats away. Which is what…no, it wasn't him; he doesn't do things like that. It was his stupid wife. Or his brainless son. I am tempted to say his boat is—of course—a plastic boat, but I will go no further than to say it is probably a plastic boat because, as I said before, woodenboatpeople are among the nicest on Earth. Even more likely, it's not a sailboat at all but a powerboat. Prejudice? Possibly, just possibly.

By then you're awake and having performed your ablutions—I wonder, could 'abluted', from the verb 'to ablute' be allowed—it's time to go through the stove and cooking routine all over again. And you sit there, enthusiastically agreeing there's nothing to beat a breakfast of half- cooked bacon and lukewarm beans, compounded with the delicate aroma of propane gas.

If you think about it for a few minutes, you conclude pretty quickly that anyone who actually pays—and everybody pays, one way or another—for the privilege of spending the weekend in a floating slum where you eat, sleep, and do everything else in constant close proximity to three or four other people, in conditions that would not be tolerated in Her Majesty's prisons is, among other things, a nauto-masochist.

The next part of this adventure—unless you fancy trying to sail out of a windless cove surrounded by tall trees—is called 'getting the engine started'. Most of the time, no problem. But there is a gremlin in every marine engine ever made. And today your gremlin pays a visit. Now I should make it clear that my life has been sadly devoid of moments of mechanical triumph. I am very comfortable working with wood; I've always assumed that this is because that was what my father did for a living. And I have a lot of power tools in my workshop and another lot in my garage that I use in the garden. But I don't get along too well with machines. Of any kind. Which is why I was thrilled to bits with myself the day I started the boat engine by hand when it did not start automatically. Actually it was only after several minutes of misery that it even occurred to me there might be another way to start it than by pressing a button and turning a key, because I remembered that when I was a boy in London I would sometimes see people starting cars by cranking the engine with a big handle.

I found the instruction book, at which I had never previously looked. And I couldn't believe it. It was, incredibly, in Japanese. Then Glynis, who was looking at the back cover, said that if I turned it over it was in English at the other end. So I did. And there were precise instructions. And it worked. First time! A real moment of triumph for a mechanical klutz. A while later, a colleague in the Bank told me about an exalted individual who had, after having engine problems on his boat one day, immediately enrolled in a marine engine course. I shall just assume it will never happen again.

It's not at all the same in North Norfolk. Fundamentally because in a thirty-foot boat there are few places you can go to and get back from in a weekend. True, you could cruise to and from Brancaster, Overy, Wells, Morston, and Blakeney. But they are so close together you can get from any one of them to any other on the same tide. They comprise what you might call a closed system. And to go farther afield presents two problems. First the places that are not too near are all too far. Second, they aren't worth going to anyway.

I suppose you could cruise from one of the Magic Kingdom ports to the ancient port of King's Lynn. But why would you want to? It's not a place for sailors. Beyond Lynn—which is to say, to the north—the nearest port is Boston. Same problem. You might say 'better than Lynn' but so what? And it's more than fifty miles. And it's in Lincolnshire. Which is like New Jersey. It's a place you pass through on the way to somewhere else. Like Yorkshire. Or the Farne Islands. Or Scotland. And forget about cruising from Norfolk to Yorkshire for the weekend. It's not only too far, it's also too cold except for a few weeks in July.

You could go the other way—to the east. And where would you get to? Yarmouth, that's where. Or Lowestoft. Oh, but you say, you can go through Yarmouth or Lowestoft to the Broads and wouldn't that be fun? The short answer is no, because a boat designed to sail well on the Broads and the rivers that link them is not the sort of boat you'd take to sea. Just as the average coastal cruiser is not ideal for sailing on the Broads. Even if the mast can be easily raised and lowered on a tabernacle, it will still have too much freeboard to get under certain bridges, such as the one at Potter Heigham. Sailing on the Broads is all very well and can be very charming though rarely exciting. But not in the sort of medium-sized cruiser you find in the creeks of the Magic Kingdom's harbours. Much better to hire one of the traditional Broads yachts or daysailors you find at such places as the County Sailing Base at Ludham.

So, in practice, there is really nowhere to go in a sailing cruiser if you've only got the weekend. If you have more time, you can of course go to lots of places. Like Holland. Or Germany. Or Scandinavia. Or for that matter the estuaries of Suffolk and Essex. The corollary is that this may not be a good place to keep a cruiser at all, unless you want to use it as a floating caravan, or if you are retired or unemployed and have plenty of time for trips of several days if not weeks.

I have, however observed that many of the cruisers regularly berthed in the North Norfolk harbours are not used as cruisers at all. They are used as daysailors. They go out on one tide and sail around the North Sea for a few hours until it is time to come in again on the next tide. Or they're used as dinghies, which is to say they go out and in again on the same tide. Now it is of course true that you can get out to sea more easily in a big boat than in a small one because they can deal better with the rough water at the harbour entrance, so you have more sea to sail on. But, I've often wondered, why do people buy boats that are not well suited to the place where they sail? For all I know, every thirty footer in Wells harbour—actually there are not that many—may have been inherited by its owner from a maiden aunt who stipulated it should be berthed there for ever. Unlikely. Perhaps it's because it's much cheaper there than in most other places; it is because there's not a lot of demand. Or maybe it's because people don't look at maps and charts before they decide they're going to moor a boat at Wells (or Brancaster, or Overy, or Blakeney). Obviously, I don't know the answer or I wouldn't be flailing around like this and I agree that none of those possibilities is really credible. What I do know is that an awful lot of cruisers sit in the harbour from one year to the next and are rarely, if ever, used. And that a lot of those that are used, are not used for the purpose for which they were designed. Going places.

Does that mean cruising or voyaging—call it what you will—has no place in the Magic Kingdom? It does not mean that. It simply means that the scale of the Magic Kingdom is such that it must be done in small boats.

There is nowhere within the waters of the Magic Kingdom you can go in a cruiser you cannot go—with advantage—in a small boat. And you can, on a very small scale, cruise from one small harbour to another, and have as much fun doing it as you can have cruising from Annapolis to St Michaels (on the other side of the Chesapeake Bay) or across the English Channel from a south coast port to France. Small boat adventures are here for the asking and in a ten or twelve footer—like Arthur Ransome's *Swallow*, or *Titmouse*, or *Amazon* or *Wizard*—you have, in my view, a perfect match between boat and cruising ground: small boats, shallow waters, short voyages. There are enough elements of risk—in crossing the bar into or out of a harbour—to make it just exciting enough without being frightening (unless, of course, you choose to do really stupid things like going to sea when all the fishing boats have stayed in port because of the weather). Use common sense though and you and your small boat should both be in their element.

Not least because there are things you can do in a small boat you can't do in a big one. One of them is to circumnavigate Scolt Head Island. You start at Brancaster Staithe or at Overy. If the former, you leave the harbour and then keep the British Isles to your right until the entrance to Overy harbour and then follow the sinuous course of Norton Creek back to Brancaster. You can, however, stop at Overy, leaving the second part of the journey until the next day. There is another 'inside passage' from Wells to Blakeney or, if you prefer, to Morston—or even Cley or to the place I know as 'White Bridges', midway between Stiffkey and Morston.

From Wells, you go not down the harbour channel but down the broad creek that runs into the quay roughly opposite where the 'Shipwrights Arms' is now falling into disrepair. Its general direction is north east, but it twists and turns as you head out towards the East Hills that lie a mile north of the quay across the marshes. In due course the creek widens. Ahead of you, a bit west of north, is a narrow creek that runs towards the backside of the East Hills, known aptly as 'Gunbarrel'. To your right, almost perpendicular to it, is a somewhat wider creek that twists away to the east. It will eventually, and long after you've pretty much decided you've somehow taken a wrong turn, lead you into open water. This creek can be sailed as long as you don't need to tack because there's not enough room for that. Which means you must have a westerly wind that, as the creek turns, will either be behind you or on your beam. Several years ago, the Wells Sharpies sailed a course that took them through the creek. They're still talking about it. Better a smaller boat. Actually better still a canoe, which you can simply pick up and carry round the twistiest bends. But, suddenly, the creek stops and there is the North Sea looking back at you.

By now the East Hills are a long way behind you. To the north there is a gentle swell. If there's not, you've chosen the wrong day. To your right (or south) there is the ragged border of the salt-marsh in its high tide mood, when it becomes, for a few hours, the edge of the world. If you have picked a day when the tide is higher than the marsh, the edge of the world will be submerged by what is known descriptively as a 'marsh tide'. Sailing *over* the top of marsh is a magical sensation. But best to do that where you are sure you know the lie of the land beneath you. And unless you do this trip often, that means not here. So press on, due east, until you have to decide which haven you are heading for.

The old grey lifeboat station on Blakeney Point is dead ahead. Your first option, before you get there, is to seek out the opening, quite close to the landward side of the marshes, that takes you—very quickly—into a tiny anchorage. There are not many boats here. A few motor cruisers. The odd sailing cruiser. And some small boats of various descriptions. There is no settlement. There is not even a road. But there is the coastal footpath that will take you to Stiffkey (heading west) or Morston (heading east) in less than half an hour. The coast road can, however, be seen in the middle distance and can be reached on foot on another path that runs perpendicular to the coast, reaching the road at one of two white painted bridges across the River Stiffkey which empties through a sluice into the little anchorage. This is, in my view, the most exotic harbour of them all. It is not the most convenient. But then, who says convenient is best? Some people call this place Stiffkey. But it is no nearer Stiffkey than Morston, and I prefer to call it White Bridges because everybody then knows where you mean.

Morston is, however, your next option. Here, the creek is much longer and it twists and turns quite a bit before taking you past a series of long gangplanks that jut out from the edge of the creek to give access to boats at high tide. A number of them belong to the ferry boats that run between Morston and the Point, pausing on the way to give their passengers a brief glimpse of the seals bobbing about on the new tide. The village is not visible from the hard and you have to go up a short—and mercifully unpaved—road to reach it. When you get there it is not very big. A pub, the 'Anchor', and a small shop next to it. A few houses. Morston Hall, which in recent years has become a country house hotel. And a medieval church. I like Morston very much, even though there's not much of it to like. One of the things I particularly like is going to the cottage at the top of the lane that goes down to the hard, to buy ferry tickets from the back door. There is a feeling of oneness in it. Of home and work being fully integrated. That is so rare now in developed countries like England. I get the same feeling in farmhouses. Except those, and there are more and more of them, which have been taken over by farm companies so there is no longer a link between the farm kitchen and the fields and the place of work is an office complex perhaps twenty miles away. I understand the economics. But I still find the old order somehow reassuring. At Morston, the old order might have had a different face if a scheme of the 1890s had materialized. Morston quay would have become a railway terminal and the village would certainly have been different had that happened, although, by now, the railway would be a relic and its business a memory.

Then there is Blakeney. The creek from the open water known as the Pit to the quay is short. It is also straight because it was cut through the marsh in 1817 to allow bigger ships—of up to 150 tons—to reach the quay. By the 1860s there were regular passenger services to and from London and Hull. But the railway did not come to Blakeney any more than it went to Morston. It went to Wells instead. Blakeney today is probably, in the eyes of most people, the better for it. It is smaller than it would have become had the railway come there. And there are no remnants of commercial buildings on the quay because none was ever built. There are houses instead. I personally think more of Wells, remnants of commercial and industrial buildings notwithstanding. But Blakeney, without issue, is the delight it is rumoured to be. It is not (quite) a small town whereas Wells is (just) a small town. It is, rather, a large village. It has quite a lot of shops though there are many things you can't buy there and the bank is only open a few hours a week. We none the less do a lot of our food shopping at Hill's in Blakeney, although—as our village shop has, over the years, widened the range of what it sells—we have bought more and more of our day-to-day needs in Binham.

There is one more option: Cley. By the nineteenth century, Cley was not the port it had once been. Fewer vessels were registered there than at Blakeney and fewer master mariners lived there.

But little more than a century ago, it was still a thriving maritime community. The voyage up the channel to Cley is rarely made these days but it can still be done. Eventually though you run out of water. Or in to deep rushes. And that is as far as you can go. When you get there, having run due east parallel to the shore and then made a sharp turn to the south, you will be looking at what was once the broad estuary of the River Glaven. The river is still there, its most-of-the-time-gentle flow controlled, like that of the Stiffkey, by a sluice gate across the road. Hard to imagine that big ships of a hundred tons and more used to sail through where you are now sitting in your small boat, up to the old and long-gone quay at Cley and farther on, to the port of Wiveton. But they did.

There are now few options for the cruising camper. Before we were married, and well before conservation interests dictated the need to prohibit camping on them, it was easy enough to take to the hills in a small boat. The East Hills that is, off Wells. One summer, around 1960, there was a season-long encampment over there with which nobody interfered and which harmed no one. And one night, not long before I was married, I took to the East Hills with my future brother-in-law, Gary, not like the owl and the pussy cat in a beautiful pea-green boat, but in the bright red canoe I had built a year or so earlier. During the night there was what Sadaam Hussein might call the 'Mother of all Thunderstorms'. We were asleep when it started. But realizing that our tent, for reasons I do not need to explain, had steel poles, I thought it might be better to leave the tent to its fate and we decamped to a makeshift shelter in a hollow on the edge of the beach. From there we watched the storm march, in three phases, along the coast. It was magnificent. Since then I have seen massive thunderstorms all over the world, including one in Mexico that I flew through the middle of in an old DC-3. But I have never seen a more spectacular storm.

It is still possible to camp on Scolt Head Island and on Blakeney Point if you have the necessary permission from the National Trust which now owns them both. But that will only be forthcoming if you can get yourself tied in to the field research programmes conducted on them by, respectively, the Geography Department at Cambridge and the Biology Department at University College, London. You can readily see why access is restricted, and this is, unfortunately, one of those situations where 'Suppose everybody did it?' *is* a valid question. It is none the less a pity that there are now too many of us with the time, the inclination, and the means to use these empty beaches and marshes for it to be ecologically safe to allow any of us to do so. The freedom to wander at will that pervades Arthur Ransome's stories about other wild places in England and Scotland—as far as I know he never visited the

Magic Kingdom and he certainly didn't write about it—has gone. For ever. Access is the issue 'of the 1990s. And it will remain an issue as long as people wish to enjoy the natural environment. Since that wish seems to me to be a constitutive part of human nature, I assume that means for ever.

None the less, it still seems to me the Magic Kingdom is a perfect cruising ground for people who want to travel slowly at little expense. A little boat for little waters, in scale with the landscape. For there is nothing (yet) to stop you sleeping in your little boat, under the stars if you like or under a boom tent if you dislike. And you don't have to fuss with cooking either, unless it is to boil some water for tea in the morning. You can find food ashore in almost all the harbours although Morston is a bit doubtful on that score and White Bridges is hopeless; but then you can walk along the coast path and find some. I wouldn't fancy doing it myself for more than an overnight stay—strange, isn't it how hot showers and clean underwear become obsessions as you get older?—but if you want the feel of voyaging and the satisfaction of leaving one harbour and arriving at another, it's all there, in miniature. It's a bit like walking. The best way to get to know a piece of country that changes many times from one mile to the next is to go on foot. That will not serve you well in places like the Arizona Desert or the Great Basin of Nevada, where the scale is enormous and you could walk for hours and still be looking at the same view. But in a piece of country as varied, as say, the Lake District or the North Norfolk coast the best way to travel is on your own two feet. Similarly, in a network of creeks and marshes you want to go slowly enough to enjoy them and not to arrive too quickly at your chosen destination. Henry David Thoreau understood that very well.

30 July

My mind contains a small, and almost unchanging, stock of loose couplets and bits of verse. Most of them have been there since I was at school. Many of them, to all intents and purposes, are anonymous. That is to say, I don't know who wrote them and, in most cases, I don't know where I read or heard them. Like bits of orphaned music that I know very well but can't put a name to, I find, every so often, that one of these stray bits of verse comes in to my mind and won't go away again. There is one there now:

So I went down to Cley,
At the end of July...

The lines about Cley are relevant because I am about to go there, tonight, to look at a house in which we might be interested. This year, for the first time, while Glynis is off in Oxford I have been looking at houses. Only a few. And what I am looking for, is what I have thought of for many years now, as our ***real*** *house. Now, that is not to say our existing house is unreal. It is tangible enough. And in its own way real enough. It is in Binham, and is part of a complex of converted barns, coach-houses, and stables that was once* *part of the adjoining property, then known as Abbey Farm. The whole lot—the farmhouse, the barns, the coach-houses, and the stables—were built around 1860, and the 'dependencies' as they are properly called, were converted over several years, starting in the 1970s. What is now our house was once a large coach-house and since we bought it from a firm of Nottingham-based developers in 1974 it has been our home in England.*

We didn't plan to come to Binham. It was just one of nine or ten villages near Wells where we looked for houses when we decided to buy. Glynis, however, knew it well, because she and her father—Glynis on her little red bicycle, her father on his big one—used to deliver newspapers here, as to other villages, after the war. It was—and, for that matter, without question still is—one of the most attractive of them all. Partly because of the magnificent ruins of the priory in the field opposite our house. And partly because it was (and is) what people call 'unspoiled'.

We have been very happy in this house. It is spacious. There are exposed beams and interesting brick and flint walls. And above where I am now sitting, the ceiling is nearly thirty feet from the floor. It has three bedrooms; two bathrooms (one of which was only added last year); and the sitting room, dining room, and kitchen areas flow in to each other through brick and flint arches. Next year, there will be a new gallery above the kitchen that will add another space for Cameron or Catriona to call their own. It does not however have a private garden. Nor is there a workshop. Nor a wine cellar. Nor several other things we do not strictly need but would none the less like to have when, in due course, I retire from the Bank and we will live here at least part of every year.

Hence, the early stages of a search—that I expect to take a long time—for our real house. And by real, I mean a house that was not born yesterday. Or even in 1860 because—while there is nothing to suggest Victoriana in our converted coach-house—neither of us likes the fussy, prissy, overelaborate style of four-fifths of the last century. There was a time when I wanted to move from Binham to Wells, to be closer to our friends there. But the more we looked, the more we realized Binham was the best place for us while we were spending most of our time in another country. No garden is a good thing when you are not there to tend it. And we actually have a very pretty garden to look at whose only disadvantage is that it is shared. Why would I want a workshop on vacation? And we're not here long enough to make much use of a cellar. But later. When all our time is our own and we can migrate from one country to another as the year passes; then we shall want those things.

So at the end of the day I'm off to Cley (I can't believe I wrote that), to see whether the house we are looking for is there. And if it isn't, it will be somewhere else in the Magic Kingdom.

The Language of Architecture

Well, it wasn't there. Quite a nice house. But almost inaccessible. Its best feature was a lovely gable end. That certainly justifies its being a listed building but it is a lot better than the rest of the house. One of the things I'm learning is that a 'listed' building may be remarkable for only one thing: a gable end, a doorway, a front wall. The rest may be quite dull. And there is an enormous difference between Grade 1 and Grade 2 buildings. Not only because there are a lot more Grade 2 buildings than Grade 1 buildings. But also because they cost much more although most of them of them aren't houses anyway.

One of the things I like best about the Magic Kingdom, and one of the things that helps define it, is what architects call its vernacular architecture. A rather good word, 'vernacular', which, when applied to language, conveys the idea of something distinctive but not unique; idiosyncratic but not arcane. What makes local buildings distinctive here is the combination of brick and flint walls and pantiled roofs.

Bricks are, of course, made everywhere. It is the flint that makes the difference. The 'Good Sands' are full of flint. Even now. Just this morning I was walking by a newly ploughed field and there was a heaped-up row of fresh dug flints along the edge. You might have thought that after being ploughed for so long the flint would all have come to the surface long ago and have been used for building. After all, there is evidence not thirty yards from where I am sitting—in the low wall around the grounds of the ruined priory—that flint has been used to make walls here since at least the twelfth century.

Flint is special because when you split it the inside is quite unlike the surface. It is mostly grey, with streaks of white and black and brown. It glistens even when dry. Flint would be a cold, hard and uncompromising material if the inside were all you could see. But because each piece has a smooth and irregularly curved profile, you can also see the softer tones of buff and cinnamon and russet on the faces it presents to the world. In our house, the flint is bordered by warm, worn red bricks. Those by what were the doors are abraded and grooved by the friction of carts, coaches, and harnesses across them during the first incarnation of this building.

Then there are the pantiles. They come in two versions, glazed and unglazed. The unglazed ones are much more common and are always a uniform deep—but not dark—red colour. The glazed variety are greyish black, the result of being fired with salt. And they are shiny, whereas the red ones are not. The special thing about pantiles is that they are asymmetrically curved, with a tighter curve on the left than on the right so that in profile they resemble a capital 'S' lying on its side with its first curlicule compressed.

As you go south from the core of the Magic Kingdom, flints and pantiles are replaced by brick. In Fakenham, you are reminded of the rural origins of flint by the fact there is very little of it in the town. To the west, there is a rather abrupt transition to the use of carrstone, a darkish red sandstone that tells me I am in West Norfolk. It is abundant around Sandringham; all the estate villages are made of it. I suspect that carrstone does not wear too well, although it quickly acquires a patina of yellow, brown, and green lichens that soon makes it lose its newness. And to the east, beyond Cley, there is a transition as the local availability of flint diminishes, and it is replaced by a jarring, jumbled mixture of this and that, without pattern or cohesion.

The outside walls of our house are at least two feet thick, and they were built—in 1860—in exactly the same way they would have been built seven or eight hundred years earlier. Again, the evidence is in the partially ruined wall of the priory across the lane. They work pretty well but even if they worked less well—and they are not, by the way, perfect; they tend to let damp through—they would still be wonderful because they have metaphorically grown out of the ground on which they stand.

That is always, to my mind, the key to whether building materials look well or not so well. The stone houses and cottages of Grasmere and Coniston look as though they had grown there and, in a sense, they did. Likewise the dry stone walls of the Pennines and the wooden clapboard houses of Castine, Maine. The yellow stone houses of Northamptonshire, the Purbeck stone of Corfe Castle and its surrounding cottages, the dark slate structures of mid-Wales and western Pennsylvania, and the adobe of upland Colombia all fit, and for the same reason.

Conversely, the granite house that looks right in the Scottish Highlands would be out of place in the Magic Kingdom. Likewise a house built of limestone or marble or even wood would look out of place and would be out of place, because those are not local materials. It is not therefore surprising that I find the handful of carrstone houses in the Magic Kingdom are wrong here; carrstone is not a local material.

I also dislike the Palladian monstrosities of Holkham and Houghton Halls mainly because they are just that. At least to my eyes. And I cannot imagine what they would look like had they been built of brick and flint. It would have been a waste of materials. They jar the landscape—or is it now the 'manscape'—not only because of their fussiness and ornateness, but also because they are made largely of imported materials. Every stone of Houghton came from a single quarry at Aislaby in Yorkshire, shipped into Wells and thence to Houghton where England's first prime minister built his Hall.

My father-in-law, who was an active member of the North Norfolk Labour Party in the latter part of its halcyon period, used to say he'd like to see Holkham Hall turned into flats for workers. A bit impractical, I always thought, though certainly well intentioned. Where were the workers anyway? But my dislike of the place has nothing to do with ideology. It is entirely a matter of aesthetics. I would not be in favour of either using it for something else or pulling it down. It has a place in the history not only of North Norfolk but of England, because it was built by Sir Thomas Coke, later the first Earl of Leicester, whose 19th century namesake became a leader of what came to be known as the Agricultural Revolution.

To demonstrate my consistency and non-partisan credentials, I should add that I also dislike small houses made of the wrong materials. In fact, since there are more of them they actually do a lot more damage to the built environment than Holkham or Houghton Halls, which are, after all, hidden away in enormous parks; at Holkham the only bit you can see for miles around is the top of a column that stands near the Hall. Just today, I have been reminded of how much damage they can do.

This morning, we went to look at a Georgian farmhouse near Sculthorpe. The grounds are splendid. But the house is not. Right next to it, in an imaginative conversion of what were once barns belonging to the farm, a Fakenham firm has recently completed its new offices. I hope they win a prize for them. They are superb. Although they are only about fifty yards from the farmhouse, they blend with it perfectly. But much farther away from it—all of two hundred yards, I should think—there are three new bungalows. Even though they are much farther away, their pink bricks and large paned windows are quite incompatible with the older building. As it happens, the house is in such poor condition that I am not remotely interested in it. But it is still painful to think that some architects can be so insensitive to the juxtaposition of old and new, and that others are apparently blind to it.

Then this evening, in Cley, at the bottom of the garden of another house I wouldn't want anyway for other reasons, there was another shrieking bungalow. I wonder sometimes about the planning process in this country. It invented town and country planning. It harnessed what I think is a peculiarly English sensitivity to the relationships between land and buildings and an awareness of the need to preserve harmony between old and new. It developed rules that are pretty draconian by the standards of most other countries. Yet the planners allow new pink brick bungalows squashed into empty bits of land to scream defiance at a Jacobean house (that's the one in Cley) that has been there a lot longer. It may have pantiles—that is to say, it does have pantiles—but in this context they are virtually a cliché. As though pantiles could redeem nasty brick and out-of-scale windows. They almost make it worse. These examples are not, moreover, isolated: the east quay in Wells is full of windows that should not be there; there is a new pink bungalow on the road between here and Warham; and although they have made a definite effort to fit in, the houses in the estate-like development on the western side of Langham don't quite make it because they have used rounded beach stones rather than flint—as a veneer over a cinder-block structure.

But what am I trying to say? Are these not trifling complaints, pernickety details almost, beside so much that is sensitive and imaginative? I am being grouchy and mean and pedantic. So there are a few errors. There are many more triumphs. Small strokes of architectural genius that together, yet quite accidentally, make the 'manscape' of the Magic Kingdom one its most enticing features. In comparative terms, what seem to be poor planning decisions in North Norfolk are, after all, minor blemishes by comparison with the travesties that mark the passage of time and the absence of thought about consequences in other places; the United States, for example, not to mention other countries that are seemingly oblivious to the quality of the built environment.

In the USA, the instances of buildings that fit well in their settings are exceptions, not rules. There are the postcard-perfect, storybook villages like Jackson, New Hampshire, and small New England towns like Edgartown, Massachusetts. As I remember them, they are made entirely of clapboard houses painted stunningly subdued tones of blue and green and red, with white spired churches that make it clear that Nonconformity and dull architecture do not have to go hand in hand. They are jewels in a crown of mostly thorns that once seen are never forgotten. It is churlish to knock America for being new. Everywhere was young once. The fact remains that in Anytown, USA, buildings are thrown together as a function of freedom to do what you like. And the result—which, thanks to ubiquitous American movies, is now familiar the world over—is usually just plain ugly.

That is not to say planned communities are necessarily better. Anyone who has been to cities like Islamabad or Brasilia, or for that matter Stevenage or Harlow, has been chilled by the tyranny of a continuous present. It is as though on some dreadful day in 1957, Kubichek, the architect of Brasilia, said, 'Let there be Brasilia', and the whole place—at least its central parts—was instantly created. Ever since, it has been decaying like rotten teeth. These cities are caught in time-warps, frozen for ever in the year of their creation. They are boring. They are dull. And they are frightening. How would you like an address like: Apartment 12, Block B, Section 45, Zone 8? Orwell would have said (in triumph), 'Told you so!' And so he did, although he certainly didn't have Brasilia in mind when he wrote *1984*. But planning—conceived not as a matter of blueprints but as guidelines (and, if necessary, rules) to curb the egregious effects of free markets—is, in my view, essential in an age of instant gratification and the rapid succession of different uses for the same piece of land.

The design of infrastructure is of course crucial: you can either see it or you can't. And it is amazing how many people are blind to the intrusion of infrastructure until they look at it through a viewfinder. What they see throughout America, and in most other countries, are strands of cables strung like so much spaghetti from poles to houses and businesses carrying electric power and telephone connexions from distribution lines to individual buildings. Why does the world's wealthiest nation not put its cables underground? If England can afford it, so can America. Why then do they choose not to do so?

I suspect it is partly a matter of ideology. Planning, control and government are all seen by mainstream Americans as necessary evils. What George Bush and Ronald Reagan before him have been saying for the last twelve years is not new; Thoreau said it better:

> I heartily accept the motto, 'That government is best which governs least'; and I should like to see it acted up to more rapidly and systematically. Carried out, it finally amounts to this, which I also believe, — 'That government is best which governs not at all.'

The radical tradition—in the conservative sense of the term—has a long and mostly honourable history in the United States. One I suspect most Americans, even those who today disown it, would salute. But they disown it now for a very important reason. When Thoreau took himself off from Concord to Walden Pond in the middle of the nineteenth century, there were not many Americans to share an enormous country. The pace of change was slow. Towns did not then sprout like magic beans, overnight (although they were soon to do so on the moving frontier of the west). In New England, and up and down the eastern seaboard, towns and villages grew slowly and organically, one house or place of business at a time. There was no need for planning regulations or zoning because people were neighbours. They knew each other. They were interdependent. And they used common sense and an inborn sense of propriety to tell them what to do with the land.

There was no need to protect the right of every American to build what he wanted to build, where and when he wanted to build it, because nobody threatened to take that right away. Simple courtesy demanded that you did not build a noisy factory in the middle of town. And in a pre-industrial age there was not much choice of building materials. Except for the very wealthy, people used what was at hand, local things. The result—to their eyes, no doubt, and in the rare cases where it has survived to ours too—was generally harmonious.

It is an altogether different matter now. Where co-operation once produced harmony, in transient societies —such as that of the United States, where almost everyone, everywhere, comes from somewhere else—and large, anonymous population centres in other countries where people do not know each other, voluntary co-operation in the form of sensitivity to the needs and feelings of other people is unusual. The result is that some kind of restraint is essential, because the untrammelled exercise of individual freedom to build as one pleases will inevitably produce disorder. If you don't believe me, go and look at the vast parking lots illuminated by neon signs and populated by shops and fast food restaurants that surround every town and city in America. They look exactly the same in Rockville, Maryland, as in Vernal, Utah. Although the vehicles are different; in Vernal the pick-up trucks have gun racks.

All human organizations have three essential elements: control, autonomy, and co-operation. As far as the built environment is concerned, co-operation was a natural state in a simpler society but is hardly natural now. So you don't have co-operation. When you have autonomy, you get Rockville Pike and Main Street and Sunset Boulevard. Nobody can really like the way they look. But nobody seems able or willing to curb the excessive consequences of almost unlimited freedom. 'Almost', because for some reason the construction codes are, if anything, more stringent in the States than in most European countries. To exaggerate a bit but not a lot, the (local) government doesn't much mind what it looks like or what it's made of, as long as you build it the right way. It's a point of view. It's a libertarian way to approach land use. But it has produced some dreadful results. Never in human history can so many otherwise beautiful places have been so wantonly spoiled by insensitivity.

There are exceptions; naturally, because generalizations like these are grounded in exceptions. Witness, for example, the ferocious battle to keep McDonalds—and, in practice, Burger King, Colonel Sanders, Wendys and all the other fast food troughs—out of Martha's Vineyard in the 1960s.

I wondered when we first went to the Vineyard why the

conservation movement was so militant. I suspected their motives; wasn't the 'Keep McDonalds Out' campaign just elitism and snobbery disguised as environmental awareness? That was before I took a good look at Cape Cod. The very name of Cape Cod is redolent with brine, oilskins, and blue skies over pristine beaches. Read John Updike's novels set on the Cape and you can smell the sea and brush the sand off your bare feet. But go there and weep, for the Cape that was there once but is certainly not there now. That, I learned, was what all the fuss was about. Today the Cape, tomorrow the Vineyard, and after that there's nowhere left. In the United States, the price of conservation, like that of freedom, is eternal vigilance.

The reluctance of most Americans to embrace planning, and their tendency to suspect government, is related to their intuitive understanding that government is largely about intent. Governments live in worlds of five-point plans and proposed legislation. And of course—whatever it is they are governing—of budgets. The English word is not nearly as good as the Spanish one, *presupuesto*, which literally means 'presuppositions' about outcomes. Presuppositions are not forecasts. They are not contracts. They are tentative estimates of what will happen to incomes and expenditures, assuming the assumptions on which the budget is based turn out to be close to the mark. They are, quintessentially, about intent.

Americans in particular suspect government because its preoccupation with intent means it is less concerned with results. And it is results, irrespective of intentions, that really matter. I think this preference is strongly linked to the way Americans take care of their historical monuments. The first summer we were there, in 1973, we went for a couple of weeks to Castine, a small town on Penobscot Bay halfway up the cold coast of Maine. It is a hauntingly lovely area, lost in mists and sea fogs where the music of time is the soulful clashing of bells on channel buoys. It is certainly a Magic Kingdom in its own right.

One of the things that struck me most, however, was the number of plaques and memorials that we found all over the little town. They told how, at different stages in its history, Castine had been occupied by the forces of half a dozen European countries, including Denmark and Holland. There was an intense pride in the past, and a sense of continuity with it, that I had never seen anywhere else.

Since then, I have seen it all over America. Nowhere more poignantly than in the Civil War battlefield memorials that are numerous near my northern Virginia home and are found as far away from it as Vicksburg, Mississippi, and Atlanta, Georgia. These battlefields are magnificently preserved and superbly interpreted for the visitor. And although I would have to say that one of them—at Gettysburg—is excessively commercialized, even there the quiet dignity and re-created horror of what happened in what southerners still call 'The War Between The States' comes vividly through.

A year or so ago, there was a quite out-of-character-fuss when a property developer wanted to create a shopping mall on part of the site of the First and Second Battles of Manassas. That, I should explain, is how they are known in the south. In the north, they are called the First and Second Battles of Bull Run. Why the difference? Because the south named battlefields after the nearest town, whereas the north named them for the nearest stream or river. And since this battlefield was in the south, Manassas it is. Conversely, go to the battlefield that could be called either Antietam (the river) or Sharpsburg (the town), and Antietam it is because that was in Maryland, a nominally northern state then and now.

Anyway, the conservationists won and there is no mall at Manassas (had there been, Battlefield Mall might have been a likely name). So, when the right bells are rung, Americans can and do get quite worked up about land use, particularly when something old is there. In fact I think they are probably more sensitive to preservation—as a conscious and deliberate choice—than they are about conservation. Contrast, for example, the charmed life of the Northern Spotted Owl and the Snail Darter as protected species with an almost complete lack of concern about the shape and form of the built environment.

Our first-year trip to Maine also showed us a distinctively American approach to what happens to the spaces around homes, generically known as 'yards'. Fastidious as they were about preserving links with the past, Americans seemed to see nothing wrong in using rural settlements as trash heaps. As we left the freeway which had brought us to the Maine–New Hampshire border, we drove north along the coast on US Route 1. The countryside, though wet on a grey Saturday morning in mid-June, was appealing. Except that every time we came to what might have been called villages but were more spread out than villages we had seen in other countries and seemed to lack shops and post offices and other conveniences, we saw run-down houses surrounded by besieging armies of old refrigerators, bits of old cars, disused baths, and other non-biodegradable junk.

It was a shock to the system. How could people be allowed—or allow themselves—to spoil otherwise restful settings? Were there no laws against turning your yard into a junkyard? In other countries, even very poor ones like Haiti and Uganda, rural areas did not look like this. Partly, of course, because in countries like those people had next to nothing and even an old car or an old refrigerator was an unimaginable luxury. But there was something else. Was it a form of blindness to the environment? A statement of despair? Or perhaps a gesture of defiance: I am wretched and I cannot get back at you so I will trash this place and spoil it for you too?

Up and down the eastern seaboard, and to the east at least as far as the Appalachian Mountains, rural America is often like that. Where there is poverty, there is usually ugliness. Those who feel cast off from society repay the compliment by littering the countryside with its cast-off consumer durables. Not everywhere, though. In the mountains of Kentucky and Tennessee, where people are statistically poorer than anywhere else in the United States, rural poverty hits you as strongly—and in context perhaps more strongly—as in the mountains of Ecuador or Kenya. But there is a difference. Perhaps they are so poor they can't afford junked cars. But it is tidier and cleaner and less abandoned looking than the Mid-Atlantic states or New England. I will not go on to talk about the simple dignity of the rural poor or, for that matter, the urban poor or the suburban poor. All poverty, wherever it occurs, degrades those who suffer it and diminishes societies that have a choice and tolerate it. Many societies do not have much choice. But there is something extraordinary about the fact that the richest and most powerful country the world has yet seen takes this sort of despoilation in its stride; look at the other side of the road, close your eyes, put the pedal to metal and move on.

The point of all this is not to knock the United States. Merely to put the transgressions of North Norfolk in a larger context. In the middle of the otherwise unspoiled Smith Island in the Chesapeake Bay, there is a literal mountain of junked cars beside the island's only road. When they stop running, their owners just push them in the marsh. Every so often a crane is brought over from the mainland to pile them higher. And there they will be until they rust which will be a long time. Beside travesties like that the nasty pink brick and oversized windows seem mere nothings. And in that perspective they are.

I believe that the contrast is not simply a matter of political attitudes towards planning—or even towards the relative values of control, autonomy, and co-operation. It seems to me that—limiting the comparison to the United States and the United Kingdom—the different treatment of the rural environment reflects something that is deeply embedded in the two cultures.

It is common knowledge that the Englishman's or woman's (I know of no gender differences) secret idyll is a country cottage with roses round the door; the only difference between one man's or woman's dream and another's is the size of the cottage which, of course, is a function of means. In the society that invented the Industrial Revolution and in which cities as manufacturing centres were born, it may seem strange that everybody thinks they want to live in the country. Nowhere else in Europe do you find that. Urban man or woman in France, Spain, or Germany wants to live in a city because that's where he or she has grown up, believing that is where civilized people live.

In most parts of the world the country is for growing things to eat. It has fewer services, smaller shops, poorer schools, lousy health care, no entertainment and, on top of all that, higher prices. The country is an amusing place to go for fresh air, for an occasional reminder of what food looks like before it becomes food, and for periodic reassurance that people in cities are superior to country people. The country is inhabited by people who were not bright enough to leave it to live in cities. In some places, like France, it even has peasants, among whom there are bound to be some contenders for the role of idiot. Country people make jam and bottle fresh fruit because they haven't understood the best jam and fruit comes from Safeway or Harrod's Food Hall. They are also given to primitive activities like shooting animals; you never see a city person shooting dogs and cats, which are just as likely to be wild as rabbits and hares are in the country; you do, however, if you live in the suburbs of Washington DC see people in cities shooting other people, but that's somehow different.

The Englishman or woman may wear a veneer of such attitudes. But the Frenchman or woman believes them implicitly. Only in England is rural life *valued* more highly than urban life. Even after umpteen generations of urban reproduction, scratch an English city-dweller and you will find a countryman (or at least a would-be countryman) trying to get out. In the rest of the world it's the other way round. The country is somewhere you (or your grandfather or his grandfather) came from; it's a place you leave, not a place you go back to, except on visits. Look at the absurdly low relative prices of rural property in France and Spain; relative, that is, to those of urban France and urban Spain and rural England. They reflect the differences in the value placed upon urban and rural lifestyles.

In the Magic Kingdom, the sustained effort over the last twenty years to find places to put new houses and bungalows and find farm buildings to convert to homes testifies to the continued fascination of the urban Englishman or woman with the countryside. Most of them, of course, are retired and the promised transition from Birmingham, Sheffield, or London is what has kept them going for the last thirty years. This is why so many places are becoming retirement communities. They are, however, quite unlike their counterparts in such southern states of the USA as

Florida or south-western ones as Arizona. Those are purpose built and are exclusively inhabited by people over fifty-five.

Whereas the Americans have ceded their countryside to the indigent, and the French have abandoned large chunks of theirs to the English, the retired English who have not gone to Provence or the Dordogne have continued to arrive in, among other places, the Magic Kingdom—some of them, I am sure, not knowing it is a Magic Kingdom. The result since the 1970s, coupled with the influx of second-home owners (which of course includes us), has been to drive a wedge between the real local population and the immigrants. That wedge separates those who work here from those who do not, either because they do not work at all or because they work somewhere else and come here only at weekends. I can't document it, but I suspect the gaps are wider than at any time in the last fifty years.

At the beginning of this century, labour-intensive, mainly arable farming was associated with rural poverty, insecurity and squalor without current counterpart. There was a well-defined hierarchy that found expression in domestic architecture. The earl lived in a hall big enough to house a whole village. The squires lived in comfortable manor houses. The rectors lived in their ten-or twelve-bedroom rectories. The merchants lived above their shops. And the rest of the world—which is to say, most people—lived in their tied cottages or the equivalent, without indoor sanitation, without running water, and without electricity. Since the average amount of living space was so low among the poor and so high among the well-to-do, there was not much in the way of middleclass housing; there was not much of a middle class anyway.

It had been that way for about two hundred years. And it stayed that way, give or take a few details, until a well-aimed bullet in downtown Sarajevo changed it, and almost everything else, for ever. Technology had made some impact on the Magic Kingdom but had not transformed it. The railway had come from Norwich to Wells in 1893, with stops (after Fakenham) at Walsingham and Wighton Halt. Another line—the West Norfolk—had gone from Wells westwards across the reclaimed marshes to King's Lynn, crossing the coast road at Dale End (between Holkham and Overy Staithe) on its way to Burnham Market. There was primitive machinery—the sort you now see in museums—for ploughing, harrowing, and threshing, but the harvest was still cut by hand and straw was still bundled in toadstool stooks, like illustrations in children's storybooks. Hedges were still trimmed and ditches were still dug slowly and without mechanical assistance. And a thousand-acre farm still employed fifty or sixty men, a full-time gardener or two, and at least a couple of domestics. It was an environment in which everyone knew his or her place.

That order had changed for ever by 1918, and Siegfried Sassoon marked its passage in his remarkable *Memoirs of a Foxhunting Man* and *Memoirs of an Infantry Officer*. He wrote about another part of England but the social transformation he described was much the same in the Magic Kingdom as in his southern countryside. Between the wars the transition continued. More mechanization on the farms. Fewer servants in the rectories and farmhouses. More young men and women migrating to find work in Norwich and London. A few more opportunities for the children of poor parents to get a halfway decent education, although Fakenham Grammar School was still a fee-paying institution.

The Second World War, which affected North Norfolk in various ways, finished the transformation process. Afterwards, the Labour government changed the rules that governed access to health care and education; innovations in agriculture meant accelerated mechanization, better crop varieties, fewer pests and diseases, and vastly greater yields. Every village grew a small crop of council houses, in some places, such as Wells, complementing those built before the war. And socially progressive taxation began the levelling process that in due course would define common denominators that transcended social distinctions.

In this brave—or not so brave—new world, architecture was for a time governed by relict features of war-time stringency. Apart from the council estates, which generally speaking were cleverly hidden from the passing wanderer, there was little new building through the 1950s and 1960s. Then came the property bubble of the early 1970s. Prices soared to levels that left mouths agape and jaws slack. Most of the demand came not from retirees but from the newly affluent in search of second homes—us among them, for by then we had bought a house in Washington and wanted to use the profit from the one we had sold in London to buy something in Norfolk. Quite a few properties, mostly small ones, were already owned by people who lived elsewhere the rest of the week and came to Norfolk at weekends. I remember a series of cute ceramic signs, hand painted at Holkham Pottery, on the cottages in Jolly Sailors Yard in Wells in the early 1960s, each telling who lived there (at weekends) and where they lived the rest of the time: Derby, Bedford, Nottingham, I recall. But barn conversions and stable conversions and conversions of other buildings with domestic or agricultural origins were still rare. Campbell and Dorothy MacCallum had just done one of the first—on Church Street in Wells—and Dick Griffiths-Jones was working on his first project, a barn conversion in Westgate, Binham.

The second boom came at the same time it came everywhere else, in the rollicking 1980s. It is not quite over, although the property market here has been as flat as it has been everywhere else since 1990. In what is now beginning to be retrospect—which means you can get far enough away from something to look it squarely in the groin —the era of yuppies and yobboes was also the era of what someone has neatly called 'burpies': boozing urban rural parasites. They sought to soak some of their usually fast-made money into, among other things, a place in the country. But whereas other waves of immigrants before them had in general adopted the rules of the existing population, the burpies have tried to introduce their own. Not since the Vikings brought havoc to the Magic Kingdom, thereafter imposing their own laws, values, and traditions, has any group of newcomers been less respectful of what they found and more determined to impose their lifestyles on those already here. To some extent they have succeeded.

In architectural terms, their major impact has been to make farm buildings still used for agricultural purposes exceptions rather than rules. Some of the conversions ennoble an already noble countryside, with long, narrow windows breaking the surfaces of high barn walls, well-placed roof lights and well-thought-out dormers. Others look terrible, but even so probably no worse than what would otherwise have become ruins in an age when their original purpose has been overtaken by modernization.

The transformation of North Norfolk's domestic architecture in the last decade is reflected in the fact that in Binham, for example—where accommodation now includes houses, cottages, and even apartments—the amount of housing has increased at least twenty per cent since 1980, while the resident population has declined and the working population has declined more.

Is there anything wrong with that? Nothing, unless one does not want to see—and I certainly don't want to see—North Norfolk in the 1990s become the equivalent of Suffolk in the 1980s and Dorset in the 1970s. Would I rather have buildings falling down for want of repair, more pubs closing, more villages becoming ghost communities? Of course not. I just want it both ways. I want the old ways to continue. I want traditions upheld. And I want people with the means to make that possible to submit meekly to the existing rules. Am I being realistic? Certainly not. There must be choices. But I none the less find myself hoping that the road improvements which will, in due course, bring dual carriageways from London to Norfolk are not finished too soon. Weekly commuters there already are. But the day I meet someone who treks from the Magic Kingdom to London and back every day, I shall weep.

1 August

I can hardly believe it: we're still here in August. That hasn't happened for twenty years because we have got into the habit of leaving Washington soon after the end of the school term—in mid-June—and have become partly June but mainly July people. As an amusing novel by Ralph Graves, who used to be the editor of the New York Times, *points out there is a big difference on Martha's Vineyard between July people and August people, and having read it, I was glad we were July people there as well as here. In Norfolk, however, I don't think it makes a damn bit of difference. We shall see though whether there are, as everybody says, more people in August than in July. I have noted a slight thickening of people in the shops and on the beaches and marshes, and in the traffic on our local roads. That means instead of going the whole length of a one-car-at-a-time road—like the one between Binham and Wighton—without meeting another car, now you might meet on average about one and a half. Not dramatic.*

I seem to be getting into a rhythm. I rely on the sun to wake me up—touching faith in its reliability in these latitudes—and that gives me an hour or so before Catriona and Cameron want breakfast. Actually, that's not quite accurate; it is really a matter of my deciding they ought to want breakfast. I suspect they would stay up in their part of the house half the morning if I let them, except when Catriona is riding early. This morning she's going at nine, so I'll have to get them down here by about eight.

Traditions

Neither Glynis nor I grew up in a family with strong traditions. Which is probably why—without having consciously planned to do so—we created them for our children. Although we never made a deliberate decision, 'they shall have traditions', as I look back to when Carey was born in Santo Domingo twenty-two years ago I can see how certain times of the year have become special. Christmas, of course. And Halloween. And Easter. And Thanksgiving, which to my mind is the most American holiday of all and the only one that stands for simplicity. And then there is the summer, which usually means being here and doing the things we do here that we have done before. Independence Day—4 July—has never been a big thing for us, mainly I suspect because we are hardly ever in the States at that time of year.

There was, however, one 4 July here in Norfolk when friends and family decided there should be a celebration. It didn't seem odd to be celebrating the independence of the United States from Britain; partly I suppose because it was so long ago, partly because the notion of the USA (as we know it) being subservient to the UK (as we know it) seems faintly absurd, and partly because I don't think we know anybody who would defend colonialism. So the party was set and I had to think of what we could contribute.

My first thought was fireworks. Now it is a very long time—nearly forty years at a guess—since I last bought fireworks in England. And it didn't occur to me they could not be bought in July. After all, people have firework displays in summer, like the never-to-be-forgotten one at Blickling Hall in July 1990 to celebrate the centenary of the National Trust. We watched that from under an umbrella as the rain poured down, thinking this could only happen in England, and remembering an earlier occasion when we had said the same thing.

The day Carey left Rugby in 1988 we spent the morning at speeches and prize-giving in the Temple Speech Room, and then went back to her house for a picnic lunch in the lovely grounds. There we all were, drinking champagne from a jereboam thoughtfully provided by another parent, while the sky—which had been dark all morning—got darker still. Then it began to rain. Not a passing shower. Nor a torrent. But steady, traditional English rain. Out came the umbrellas and everyone continued eating and drinking, saying; 'I'm buggered if I'm going to move'. And no one did. I shot some video.

Anyway, just try buying fireworks in England in July without a licence. It can't be done. The shopkeepers I tried in both

Fakenham and Norwich obviously wondered if they should turn me in. My second idea was the Stars and Stripes. It was to be an outdoor party so I thought a flag would be very appropriate. The reaction from shopkeepers was only mildly less suspicious. Clearly , there wasn't a lot of demand for foreign flags in Norfolk. Then I had a brilliant idea. The US Air Force was still operating out of Sculthorpe, near Fakenham. So I rang them up and asked if they could lend me a US flag. They were very polite but said, 'We've only got one and it's up the flagpole.' I didn't think that could be true; they must have spares. Probably a dozen at least. The point was they didn't lend them to foreigners.

Two strikes: one more and I was out. I thought we just might have a small flag in our storage area in Binham, so I rummaged about and found it; it was very small. So I ended up wrapping it around a bottle of Jack Daniel's Black and took that to the party. As it turned out, it rained anyway.

Christmas has become, for our family as, I suspect, for many others, the most consciously traditional time of all. To the extent that by now the sequence of events is so strongly defined from the morning of Christmas Eve (when Catriona becomes St Lucia, complete with candled mantle) to the evening of Boxing Day (when we pack for our ski trip to New Hampshire the next morning) that it requires true courage for one of us even to hint about changing something. The joy is in the repetition. In the confirmation that some things, at least, are constant. In remembering other Christmases that were exactly the same and yet different, because we are all older now; and because, although it is the same house, its textures, colours, and lighting effects are continuous experiments and it therefore provides a changing stage. Christmas is both reassurance and excitement, a magical blend of old and new.

In my experience, most Americans are allergic to long, European-style vacations; doctors and lawyers and business executives just don't take a month off every summer. But I think they make generally better use of seasonal traditions than the English. Many of them were of course English in the first place and Carey and Caitlin tell me that some of them are now being reimported. As a child, I had no idea what All Hallows Eve was all about and I had never heard of Halloween. Now, at least in some parts of Britain, pumpkin lanterns and trick or treating are making a modest comeback. I didn't know about Easter egg hunts, or egg rolling either.

I think Americans are not only better at remembering traditional holidays than the British, they are also better at celebrating them. The British have a genius for formal ceremony. The Americans have a genius for public informality. Nobody does processions better than the British. They fit perfectly in a rather formal society. But put an American high school marching band in an English carnival parade and what happens? It looks ridiculous; people laugh. In fact, transport a complete Fourth of July parade from Anytown, USA, to an English town of comparable size and the effect—naïve and folksy—would make English spectators uncomfortable.

Our Norfolk traditions are a bit different. When I look back, there was, of course, a period when we were unwittingly creating them. It seems now, that in those years, the early and mid-1970s—as we scurried around the countryside, the marshes, and the foreshore, getting to know new places and defining our version of North Norfolk—we found we wanted to do certain things and visit certain places time after time. So our traditions were born, and the (now long) list took shape. There are always new things, of course. There still are; a year does not pass in which we fail to discover at least two or three things that, even after all this time, are new to us. And I don't just mean new restaurants or new pubs, which are usually new only in the sense they are under new management. I mean also places that are new because we have never been to them before at certain times of day; at dawn or in the evening, for example. And there are sometimes new tracks or paths we had previously overlooked.

But it is the familiar things which dominate our waking hours that are our traditions. I dare say a psychologist might tell me they denote compulsive behaviour; so be it. I rather prefer the notion that when we go around the Magic Kingdom, saying 'Hello' here and touching base there, we are really behaving a bit like other animals who have distinctive ways of keeping in touch with territories; we do not, of course, leave any trace of having been there.

There were, for a time, elements of ritual in the way we spent our time in the Magic Kingdom, some of which have, thank goodness, been cast aside. One in particular got heavier and heavier until it became literally insupportable. There was a time when, flush with passion for the Magic Kingdom, I would try to insist we went everywhere and did everything, each time we came. That meant, among other things, that we should walk the whole length of the coastline each summer. Not all at once, but in several stages.

It is only twenty-three miles from Brancaster Staithe to Cley. Not a long way. In fact it could easily be done in one day by the purposeful-looking walkers complete with emergency food packs, sleeping rolls, and compasses who, in increasing numbers, tackle the Norfolk Coast Path as though their objective was the other side of Antarctica. Although I can't imagine why they need all that stuff; I am sure they could walk the whole distance before breakfast without stopping.

It sounds ridiculous to say that fitting a twenty-three-mile walk into a month was sometimes difficult. But then there were some special conditions. One was we that, in the early years, we should do everything *en famille*. Another was that Carey was four and Caitlin two when we settled in Binham,and since Cameron is now only ten we have always had, until recently at least, one small person. Then there was the fact that walking along the coast was not just a matter of walking from one place to another. It all had to be done in circuits. That meant in practice, walking along the beach or the foreshore in one direction and along sea defence walls or the backs of the marshes in the other. That is to say, double the one-way distance, which meant in some cases a round trip of less than four miles but a good deal more in others. More significant than the distance was the fact that in many places you can only get to the foreshore at low water, which means—if you plan your walk around lunch, which we always do—those trips are only feasible half the time you are there.

There were, however, some circuits which had to be timed to begin on high tide in one place and have us somewhere else by low water. The circuit of Scolt Head Island, for example, requires that you take Mervyn Nudd's ferry across from the hard at Brancaster Staithe and reach the other end of the island several hours later, by which time you can walk across Norton Creek and then get back to the Staithe along the path that tops the bank between the freshwater and saltwater marshes. It is much the same at Blakeney. You take Bean's or Temple's ferry from Morston across to the landing place near the old lifeboat house. From there you walk slowly along the shingle ridge until you reach the Coastguard Station at Cley from which there is a path back to the coast road which you follow through the village as far as the mill, just beyond which there is another path along the bank that takes you in a big curve back to Blakeney and Morston.

Then there is perhaps the most important constraint of all. These excursions *must* be done in fine weather. The sky must be blue. There must be white, not grey, clouds. There should be some breeze but not too much (having experienced both, I can certify that a sandstorm on the foreshore here is remarkably similar to a sandstorm in the Arabian desert). And it should be warm enough to wear shorts but not so hot you are uncomfortable. In vintage years—1975, 1976, 1990, and 1991, for example those are not tall orders. But vintage years are infrequent.

Finally, you sometimes have other things to do. Like shopping in Norwich, which by tradition is on the first Monday after we arrive, and begins with (what I am prepared to argue are the world's best) hamburgers at Captain America's near the market place. Or visiting friends. Or walking somewhere else, because one of the joys of the Magic Kingdom is that it is countryside as well as seaside. Or rubbing brasses. Or visiting houses with an option to buy them. Or, of course, sailing.

So there are, when you take them all into account, quite a lot of things that can come between you and the realization of a modest ambition to walk from Brancaster Staithe to Cley in the course of a month: short legs and their tendency to go off in the wrong direction; tides; the weather; competing demands on time; and, of course, what economists call 'intervening opportunities'.

The exploration stage and the obsessive stage are now behind us. But I sense that the development of a physical relationship with the land—as with the water—of the Magic Kingdom was an essential part of getting to know it. Again, love is intimacy and you cannot, I think, love the saltmarshes without having at various times been covered in their mud from head to foot. You cannot love Scolt or the Point without having wandered all over them from east to west and north to south. You cannot love the fragile boundary between the domain of the soil and the domain of the sea unless you have seen it in fair moods and foul, in winter white and in full summer, on foot and at a leisurely, plenty-of-time-for-stopping pace.

But once you have done all those things, you reach a stage at which you can see them, smell them, and hear them without being there. And not just in general; in detail too. So the compulsion to rush off exploring and revisiting places you have been to before gradually fades. In a human relationship, you reach a point where you know someone very well. You can be alone with them for hours and find as much companionship in silence as in conversation. You don't take him or her for granted but none the less feel the relationship is completely secure. So it is that a place you love and know—because knowledge is a condition of the true love of places—is there for you today, and will be there for you tomorrow and for ever. So if, this year, you don't visit certain corners of the Kingdom, no need to worry. If somehow you don't walk around Scolt Head Island, you can always do it next time. Inevitably, though, in a fine summer like this one, you will find glorious opportunities to match perfect days with perfect ways to spend them. Yesterday, for example.

The tide was already falling when we left home and drove cross-country to Burnham Norton. We left the car in a grassy clearing at the bottom of the semicircular lane that leaves the coast road beyond Burnham Overy Staithe and loops back to it less than a mile farther on. The weather met all my stringent conditions as we crossed the stile and headed north over reclaimed marshes through grazing cattle. Between last time we were here and this time, English Nature has put up signposts on footpaths all along the coast, and inland too, showing the way to those who don't know it and reminding those who think they do but wouldn't be caught dead carrying a map. There was one of those signposts on the stile. Next to it there was another new sign which belonged jointly to the Holkham Estate and the Burnham Norton Wildfowlers Association. Its purpose was to provide fair warning—to anybody who might need to be warned—that the shooting rights on Norton Marsh were privately owned and that their privacy would be enforced. With guns? I wondered. Presumably not.

There used to be another sign there which said much the same thing although it didn't mention the estate. And it always put me in mind, as it did this week, of Norton Marsh in winter, when otherwise peaceable men—and, I presume, women—set out to blast birds from the sky. I am actually much more ambivalent about doing that than my last sentence might suggest, although to be honest I could not, under any circumstances I can imagine, see myself shooting any living thing. However, without remorse, I eat things that other people have shot.

Then there is the fact that while Captain Blunschli in Shaw's *Arms and the Man* was talking about weapons for a duel rather than for hunting duck, his choice of a machine-gun seems equally applicable to shooting birds. Much more efficient, one would think. Indeed, in the last century, hunters on the Chesapeake Bay actually used multi-barrelled guns mounted on punts to blast dozens if not hundreds of duck and geese out of this world in one discharge. Those guns were eventually banned not only because they were killing too many birds, but also because they were unfair. I realize I am being perverse, but it is the 'unfair' bit that, at least on one level, puzzles me.

For the same reason, I have always had some difficulty understanding why it was decent to blow people up with bombs or shoot them with bullets or disembowel them with bayonets but unacceptable to poison them. Indeed those aspects of the Geneva Convention have always struck me as unreal. War is war is war. And violence is violence is violence. I suspect the rules of what is, by definition, an uncivilized activity were drafted by men whose firm ideas about cheating had been thoroughly learned at English schools, who saw little difference between the playing field and the battlefield. But if your purpose is to kill the enemy, why does it matter how you do it? And why, one might ask, should that not apply to hunting too?

It is now a long time since I have been in the Magic Kingdom in the winter when the duck and the geese are here. And I have never been on Norton Marsh when there was frost on the pools left over from the tide, the ground crackled underfoot, and the wildfowlers were in their element. And despite my own unwillingness to do what they do and despite my perverse ambivalence, I am actually glad they do what they do. I am glad there are people who continue an ancient, indeed primitive, tradition because it is part of this countryside and has always been that way and because it is my role to adjust to it, rather than to try to change it. I would only go so far as to say the slaughter should not be excessive, but that, I would have thought, was common sense...

There is a splendid book by Alan Savory, called *Wildfowler*, which makes it abundantly clear that this avocation is usually pursued under extraordinarily harsh conditions at hours when most people are still in bed. Quite often, all for nought. Savory's book is actually about Morston, not Norton, but it offers a vivid picture of what the wildfowlers do when they go wildfowling. There is a complementary account of what happens on the other side of the Atlantic in James Michener's novel, *Chesapeake*. Like all Michener's books it begins with creation—in this case the creation of the Bay—and ends with contemporary events, which, in the case of *Chesapeake* includes the impeachment and resignation of Richard Nixon. I find these accounts fascinating, just as I find the carved wooden decoys traditionally used for duck and goose hunting up and down the east coast, from Maine to the Carolinas, fascinating and beautiful expressions of local culture.

Cold temperatures and frost on the ground were hard to picture yesterday morning as we walked across Norton Marsh. In the past, we have collected wild flowers in places such as these. But this time I took photographs with my new Japanese camera which has a macro zoom that lets me get within inches of the flowers without harming them. Photographs have the further advantage that they stay bright while the flower stays put. Much the same applies to butterflies. There was one summer when, enthused by a colleague in the Bank who had drawers full of dead lepidoptera (in his house, not his office), I made a butterfly net and we went chasing around the greens in hot pursuit of these gorgeous insects. Fortunately it was a lot harder than I expected it to be, which saved me the trauma of pinning the things on boards because the few that we actually caught were shredded in the process of extracting them from the net.

Yesterday, stopping every so often to take close-ups, we ambled along until we got to a sort of 'T' junction with the path that runs along the southern side of Norton creek, beyond which is the low bulk of Scolt Head Island. To the west, about three miles away, was Brancaster Staithe. We went east, following the bank until we slipped down on to the marsh. At that point there were three choices.

One was to cross the Burnham harbour channel and, once on the other side, to head east, either along the beach or along the edge of the marsh, to the boardwalks that lead to the path that runs along the sea defence bank to Overy. That is by far the longest route and not, in my view, the best one.

We did not take it.

We took the second route, which was the path that runs in a more or less straight line, down the western side of the channel to Overy harbour. From there, you wade across, taking care to watch what other people are doing because local knowledge of the harbour channel may not be useful from one year to the next, and since we had not walked across there this year yet, watch we did. The path itself was quite wet because there had been high tides the last couple of days. And there was one humongous hole next to a short footbridge. It was obviously full of water but it wasn't obvious that it was about two feet deep. Catriona took a dirty bath.

Overy harbour is rightly famed as one of the most picturesque places in the Magic Kingdom. It is dominated by the Boathouse which stands, sentinel-like, beside the road, looking north across the marshes to the sea. The Boathouse has been run, for as long as I can remember, by Peter Beck, who keeps one eye on his chandlery and the other on what is happening outside. The fact that it is the favourite place of so many people, and that it must be very high on the local list of most painted places, makes no difference: I am very fond of it too. And we live with it in America because an etching of the Boathouse by Nick Barnham hangs in the study in McLean. It is, without question, the heart of Overy Staithe.

The field behind the Boathouse is crammed with dinghies of all sorts and for three years, until last May, was also a shipyard. The *Overy Big Boat* was built there, all sixty feet of her. Designed and constructed by one of Peter Beck's sons and two fellow-graduates in naval architecture from Newcastle, the *Big Boat* has finished its trials on the Broads and is being chartered on the Solent to raise funds for the round-the-world voyage which is scheduled to start next year. I love the fact that less than fifty yards from where the *Big Boat* was built is the former home of Captain Woodget, the last Master of the *Cutty Sark*, who retired to Overy and spent his last years testing his seamanship against the twists and turns of the Burnham harbour channel, just as young Horatio from the rectory at Burnham Thorpe must have done more than a century earlier. This place looks like small-boat heaven. And so, in a way, it is. But it has lingering ties to blue water.

On sunny summer afternoons, there is usually an ice-cream van at the bottom of East Harbour Way. An obligatory stop. And when we were there yesterday, I had an ice-lolly—the first, I should guess, for at least thirty-five years. At that frequency, it was probably my last. Past the Boathouse, the road becomes West Harbour Way. You follow it round until it meets the coast road again, and there is a pavement—or sidewalk if you will—that now continues as far as the point where a path runs inside the hedge and along the side of what is, this year, a barley field. Just about opposite Overy windmill, the path angles across the field towards Burnham Norton. At the other side there is a stile where the path meets the sea defence wall. To left and right there are deep ditches where the River Burn runs through a sluice and into the freshwater marshes.

The road not taken yesterday—the third option—is, in my view, much the best, but the children wanted to go across the marsh so we did. Instead of taking the path over the marshes down to the harbour, you simply walk down the channel, over the sands, wading here and there through shallow water but staying clear of the deeper water near the groynes that have been built to prevent silting. There are always some people pushing or towing small boats back to the hard; there is not enough water to sail or even row and certainly not enough for an outboard. They went up on the tide in the morning knowing they would go back this way in the afternoon. There are a couple of places where you can go wrong. But here as elsewhere, just watch what others do when uncertain and it works out fine.

Whichever of the three endings you choose, you come eventually to the harbour and from there on, the route is identical. It would, of course, be possible to do this circuit in reverse. But we nearly always seem to do it in a clockwise direction. Whichever way round, the tide must be falling when you start. Just one thing. If you take the channel route through the water, don't be tempted to take a short cut across the mud. Caitlin did that once, in I should think 1977 or 1978, despite what I might now describe as some energetic advice not to do so. She was wearing green wellies that day. The wellies are still there.

3 August

Glynis came back from Oxford yesterday, her mind improved—she says—by two intensive weeks of exposure to international education. I admire her fortitude, for having just completed a school year to have then plunged into new learning. The last two weeks, being alone here with Catriona and Cameron, have been wonderful because I have had them—as I rarely do—to myself. But it is lovely to have her back.

To a much greater extent than I imagined, writing this is fun. In fact it's almost painless. Certainly, I am finding I can concentrate with a lot of distractions I could not deal with if I were writing about organization and management issues. Right now, for example, I am sitting at one end and she is sitting at the other end of the very long table we had made by Norfolk Country Craftsmen the last time we were here. The washing machine is rumbling away in the kitchen. And Cameron has just asked me if I remember I promised to hang some of his model aircraft against the roof-light upstairs. Another thing I can't explain—and he can't either—is why all his models are of Second World War aircraft. Apt, however, I suppose, because many of the planes he has modelled flew from and to the airfields of the Magic Kingdom that were created, between 1940 and 1943, where wheat, barley, and sugar beet had grown the season before.

The Astrodome

There is a rhyme that goes:

He who would Old England win,
Must at Weybourne Hope begin...

Not much better—as poetry—than the lines about Cley, I suspect although who am I to judge? But as a statement of historical fact it is reasonably accurate because, off Weybourne, there is deep water almost up to the beach. For an invader that advantage would be somewhat offset by the fact that Weybourne Hope is a promontory. Not a big one. But the cliffs are high enough to give a defender a position from which to cover the beach with fire. Or, when the Danes and the Saxons and the Normans turned up, chunks of flint or whatever they used to discourage invaders. Not that they did them much good. Just as well or we wouldn't have those Saxon churches to drool over.

East of Weybourne, and within the Magic Kingdom, there is shallow water all the way up to the beach. And apart from the low hummocks of sand at Wells, there is no protection for the defender. That reality was, of course, one of the foundations of Erskine Childers's *Riddle of the Sands*—a rare example of a story that lost nothing in transition from book to film—because this was to have been the site of the Kaiser's barge-borne invasion. It was also, quite clearly, in the minds of the military planners in the Second World War because the beaches of the Magic Kingdom were heavily encrusted with barbed wire, mines, and other obstacles and devices. The last remnants of barbed wire were still there rusting away when I first came here in the early 1960s, and some of them lingered at the edge of the marshes until quite recently. But the most visible existing reminders of the Second World War are the pill-boxes dotted around the countryside near the coast. They are overgrown now with bindweed and grasses and some of them have partly caved in. But many have survived for fifty years and I suspect they are about to become twentieth-century ancient monuments. Although they lack everything in terms of architectural merit, and are perhaps as close as we could get to the ultimate utilitarian building, they should, in my opinion, be preserved as reminders of a recent time when this peaceful landscape was anything but peaceful.

Despite the risk of seaborne invasion, the Army was not much in evidence here in the war. There were camps at Stiffkey and (a bit outside the Magic Kingdom) at Muckleburgh, the remains of which can still be seen. At Stiffkey, the old wartime huts are now part of a camp site. And down on the marshes there are two other things that countless visitors must have seen and puzzled over. One of them is the remnant of a wood and metal track across the marshes on what was then, and is now, one of the easiest access ways to the foreshore. It was laid to allow half-tracked vehicles and guns to be taken out there. The other is a circular concrete pad at the edge of the marsh between Stiffkey and Warham where air gunners in training learned to shoot target planes, launched from this pad, out of the sky.

There are less visible reminders too. It is hard to imagine that Langham Hall was requisitioned by the Army as a hospital, mainly to serve sick and wounded airmen from the local Coastal and Bomber Command stations. But the reinforced and tarmacked driveway and turning area, and the narrow extension at the back of the house that made it possible to get stretchers up and down stairs are proof enough that it was.

Despite its intense relationship with the North Sea, there was little naval activity either. From time to time, there were motor gun boats and motor torpedo boats at Wells, but the tidal range that makes it impossible to get into or out of the harbour for half the time also made it impossible to use larger vessels there—or anywhere else between Lynn and Yarmouth.

For the Magic Kingdom, as for most of East Anglia, it was above all an air war. Within it, there were four RAF stations: at Langham, Little Snoring, North Creake, and Sculthorpe. And just beyond it, there were others: at Docking and Bircham Newton to the west; at West Raynham and Great Massingham to the south; and at Weybourne to the east. After the war, one of these stations (Sculthorpe) became a major USAF base. But during the war this area lay outside the operating perimeter of the Eighth and Ninth US Air Forces. Much to Cameron's disappointment, this was not *Memphis Belle* country.

Three of the RAF's commands—Bomber Command, Coastal Command, and Fighter Command—operated, at different times, from Langham, Little Snoring, North Creake, and Sculthorpe. At the end of the war, all but Sculthorpe were put on what was then known (and may still be known, where applicable) as 'care and maintenance' status. Langham and Little Snoring were briefly reactivated in the 1950s but were returned to civilian ownership in 1961 and 1958 respectively. Sculthorpe was briefly inactive between 1945 and 1948, but on one scale or another has been operational ever since. Earlier this year, however, in the context of post-Cold War defence strategies, it was announced that Sculthorpe too will finally close.

The fields of what was, for a time, RAF Langham, just up the little road to Cockthorpe from Binham, have long since reverted to growing sugar beet, barley, and wheat. And most of the old buildings, plus a lot of new ones, have become turkey-breeding houses. The old control tower now houses the turkey farm's offices. But the most interesting building is a strange dome, about twenty feet high, that sits alone beside the Cockthorpe–Langham road, its once black-painted shell now chipped and peeling like a dermatologist's nightmare. It is an astrodome. There were never many of them and very few now remain in Britain. Its purpose was to teach navigators astronavigation and every time I pass it I wonder if it really worked. It also occurs to me, however, that I would have a hard time finding out. Where would I find the ex-navigators who once spent hours on end shut up in the dark in an astrodome on the edge of a wartime airfield in North Norfolk? How many would still be breathing?

A light aircraft that belongs to Andrew Taylor, a Binham farmer who likes to fly, still uses the runway at Langham. And a red navigation light still shines at night at the edge of the old runway. But it is eerie, crossing the taxiways and runways and hard standings that fifty years ago were rolled over by Beaufighters, Henlys, Defiants, Swordfishes, Ansons, Wellingtons, Barracudas, and later —in the 1950s—by Mosquitoes and Vampire jets. I find it hard to reconstruct in my imagination a time when hundreds of airmen lived on and around RAF Langham and the Chequers, here in Binham, and the Bluebell in Langham were their local pubs.

Just two years ago, though, there was a violent echo of the past and once again—for a moment—the Chequers was full of airmen, after an F-111 bomber, property of the United States government, crashed in the field that lies just west of our carport and opposite the priory. The pilots ejected safely and came down at Copy's Green on the Binham side of Wighton. Wilf Foyers, who owns the Crown Hotel in Wells and who was first on the scene, tells what is perhaps the only funny part of this drama. As it happened, an ambulance had just stopped at Copy's Green to pick up an elderly lady for her weekly trip to the outpatients' department in Norwich. She was unceremoniously dumped and the pilot and navigator were loaded in the ambulance instead. Too good a case to miss. After all, F-111 aircrew don't come hurtling out of the sky to land at Copy's Green very often. In fact I should say the odds for it ever happening again approach infinity.

A couple of hundred yards to the east and we would not have had a house any more. A similar distance to the north and England might have lost an ancient monument just before it celebrated its ninth century. Aptly, the *son et lumière* pageant devised for the 900th birthday festivities the next year ended with a section on 'The F-111 Miracle'. The US Air Force was extremely efficient after the crash. The village was cordoned off. Almost all the bits of wreckage were collected (the bits that were not collected had already been collected by people not in uniform) and a month later, when we arrived, it was almost impossible to tell anything had happened. I know of at least one little boy who numbers a piece of what might be called 'the true F-111' among his treasures.

For most of the war, Langham was the home of what became known as the Langham Wing of RAF Coastal Command and was the source of bomb and torpedo attacks on enemy shipping in the North Sea. Late in 1944, the Beaufighters of 489 and 455 Squadrons were replaced by the Wellingtons of 524 Squadron and an eclectic assortment of reconnaissance aircraft flown by 521 Squadron that was still there when the war ended.

Today, the only aircraft in the skies, apart from small planes, are either so high they can be heard but not seen—sonic booms are commonplace—or so low over the North Sea you could wave—or shake a stick—at the crew, were they not going so fast. Most of them are from Sculthorpe, some are from Lakenheath and Mildenhall, miles away on the Norfolk–Suffolk border. Now, Sculthorpe is to close. There is talk of converting the airfield to commercial use. The economics are suspicious. It is (thank God) far enough from major cities to be irrelevant for passenger traffic—even, I suspect, as a replacement for the now-too-small airport that serves Norwich, which until 1960 was RAF Horsham St Faiths. And if anybody thinks they could use it for cargo without rebuilding the road network of North Norfolk, they have—to use a favourite phrase of my grandmother—another think coming.

4 August

There are—as an American sailor would be apt to say—about twenty knots of wind today. Too much for us, I think. So instead of going sailing we shall take a picnic to the pine woods behind the beach between Wells and Holkham. It's extraordinary how places like that are relatively empty, even in fine weather in August. Of course, there will be plenty of people on Wells beach, trying to keep out of the sharp westerly breeze—which will be difficult, because the beach runs pretty much from west to east. And there will be a lot of people at Holkham Gap too.

At both places, you can park nearby. Near Wells beach there is parking at the bottom of the beach road that runs for a mile from the town to the caravan site near the lifeboat house. Most of the caravans there are 'static' as the English say. In the US, they would be called 'trailers'. Maybe 'immobile homes' would be an even better name for them as a counterpoint to 'mobile home'. But these static caravans are clearly not intended to be moved very often. Sometimes you see them, sitting four feet off the ground, on a flatbed truck carrying a sign that says 'wide load'. They look out of their element, just like a boat does, but somehow much more ungainly and awkward.

When a boat is sitting on a rood trailer you can, after all, see the underbody that is usually hidden below the waterline, and appreciate the curves of the hull. Naturally, some boats look a lot better than others in these circumstances. To my eyes at least, a full-keeled boat out of the water looks much better than a fin-keeled boat, whatever people may say about relative sailing abilities. But a mobile home or static caravan looks like what it is, a prefabricated and inexpensive house that is being moved from one place to another.

As we know, you don't have to design houses to be moved around on flatbeds to move them around. I might be wrong, but I fancy the people who designed and built London Bridge would be a bit surprised to learn it is now sitting in the Arizona desert, having been taken apart stone by stone and shipped there in the 1970s. And I know an American (whose name I had better not mention) who has several homes, among them an Elizabethan manor house that he purchased and had moved from Warwickshire to New Jersey. It looks ridiculous but he thinks it looks wonderful. Like the builders of London Bridge, its original builders would I imagine, be mildly dismayed to see it now.

There was also a lady of mature years (I thought of writing, 'There was an old lady of Wells', but I can't do limericks and anyway it would be out of place) who had her house in Hertfordshire dis-assembled, and then spent several years living in a caravan (not a static one either) at the bottom of her new garden in Wells while she tried to put it together again. Sadly, it got the better of her.

At Holkham, you can go to the end of Lady Ann's Drive, an extension of the road that leads from Holkham Hall to the beach at Holkham Gap. For a small sum of money you can park on the grass at the side of the drive. By lunchtime today, it will be full all the way back to the coast road, and those who get there late will have to walk about three-quarters of a mile to the boardwalk that goes across the dunes to the beach.

We shall go neither to Wells nor to Holkham. Instead, we'll leave the car on the roadside at the end of what we call a 'drift', an unmade road, wide enough for farm vehicles, that is part of a network of unmade roads that intersect the reclaimed marshes. We shall be walking on history.

The Giant of Giant Castle

When I did O-level history at my grammar school in London in the 1950s, I recall that the textbook we used attributed the Agricultural Revolution to two men, both as I now know from North Norfolk although I don't think that point was made, and if it was I have forgotten about it: Squire Coke of Holkham and Turnip Townshend of Raynham. I also remember (yet another) stanza which neatly summarized the process of enclosure that preceded what were, by the standards of the times, extraordinary changes in arable farming in this area in the late eighteenth and early nineteenth centuries:

The law locks up the man or woman,
Who steals a goose from off the Common,
But leaves the greater villain loose,
Who steals the Common from the goose.

At the time, I must have been deeply impressed by the economy of those lines (although at age fifteen I would not have put it that way), or I would not remember them now. Certainly, they capture the dilemma of the day, one we might now interpret as a matter of trade-offs between making more effective and productive use of the land through enclosure, and preserving the traditional freedoms of rural England, efficiency be damned.

The last enclosure in Norfolk was at Saxlingham in 1873; the first, a century earlier. The process was most intensive in the first and second decades of the nineteenth century when the common lands of more than two hundred parishes were enclosed by landowners eager to capitalize on the marketing opportunities offered by the war with France. Before the middle of the century, more than eighty per cent of the grazing land that had been bequeathed in or before the Middle Ages to common use was ploughed under. By 1844, only twenty-seven thousand acres of common grazing were left in the whole county, much of which thereafter survived until it was requisitioned during the Second World War. Today, there are fewer than eight thousand common acres in Norfolk and only a small part of these—such as the oddly shaped Cockthorpe Common (which lies between Binham and the sea) across which Glynis and I walked yesterday—is in the north.

As early as 1767, Arthur Young, describing the landscape of what he christened the 'Good Sands', wrote ecstatically about the 'spirit of improvement' that, in the space of a few years, had transformed 'the boundless wilds and uncultivated wastes, inhabited by scarcely anything but sheep' into 'enclosures, cultivated in the most husband-like manner, richly manured, well peopled, and yielding a hundred times the produce that it did in its former state'.

Coke of Holkham—or more precisely Thomas Coke—and Townshend of Raynham were by no means the only landowners and tenant farmers to innovate in the land of the 'Good Sands'. But they were, with Sir John Turner of Warham, the largest landowners in North Norfolk; and Coke, it is fair to say, was the acknowledged leader who would, in due course, become the 'fairest of the fair'.

By the time of the Napoleonic Wars, the Coke family—which had owned a sizeable piece of the Magic Kingdom since the Middle Ages, but had yet to become earls of Leicester again, (the title having lapsed in the eighteenth century)—had title to more than forty thousand acres of highly productive arable and pasture land. A convincing accomplishment. But it had not come without cost, and at the end of his long life Thomas Coke would lament:

> It is a melancholy thing to stand alone in one's own Country. I look around; not a house to be seen but my own. I am Giant, of Giant Castle, and have ate up all my neighbours.

As the real income of the Coke estates doubled in the wartime environment, many of the farms that even today stand out by virtue of their fine dwellings, impressive barns, and purpose-specific outbuildings and dependencies were vastly improved: Waterden Farm on the road from Wighton to North Creake was one of them; Leicester Square Farm on the Fakenham Road in South Creake was another; Egmere, hard by what would become, more than a hundred years later, RAF North Creake, a third. But the most spectacular farm of all, enthusiastically described in the 1790s, as a 'perfect paradise' by two visiting farmers from the south of England was the Estate Farm itself.

By the time innovation began in earnest on the Holkham farms, their physical boundaries had been set for more than a century. But the fertile fields behind the dunes that back the beaches between the Burnham harbour entrance and Wells, and that lie behind the sea defence banks between Wells and Cley, had been saltmarshes until they were reclaimed, in stages, by the Coke and Turner families between 1630 and 1770.

The *idea* of reclamation was undoubtedly developed by the Cokes and the Turners, but the *techniques* of reclamation came from Holland. So did the engineers who designed and supervised the construction of the embankments and drainage ditches that were the instruments for converting salted soil to freshwater fields. In a permanent sense, it all began when Sir John Coke reclaimed 360 acres at Holkham in 1660 and nearly seven hundred more early in the next century.

But the first reclamation effort was made a few miles further east, by Sir John Calthorpe. In 1637, he constructed a great bank between his home at Wiveton Hall and the quay at Cley, which was then midway between the church and the now sailless windmill. His purpose was to reclaim the lower Glaven valley, then a tidal inlet all the way up to Wiveton. It is pretty hard to build something like a sea wall without attracting attention and, once they realized what he had in mind, his neighbours were more than a bit upset. They said the bank would cause siltation which would mean the end not only of Wiveton but also of Cley as a port. Calthorpe eventually stopped construction and pulled down what he had finished. But his neighbours were quite right. In the early nineteenth century another bank was built, protests notwithstanding, and it was remarkably few years before Cley was Next-the-Sea no longer.

After Caltholpe's bank had been dismantled, nearly a hundred years passed before Sir John Turner decided to build a bank across the marshes east of Wells. The effect was quick and dramatic. Until then, a tidal inlet flowed around the slightly elevated eastern side of the town where the Northfield Estate is now, into an anchorage known as Church Haven where the marshy area known as Ramm's Marsh—so called because for many years it belonged to Charlie Ramm, the butcher—is today. It is hard to imagine now that the area bounded by the churchyard to the south, the houses on Church Plain to the west, and the large Georgian building known as Marsh House to the north was once an ocean terminal of sorts; and that the low ground to the east, where the old railway station now houses a pottery, was a channel to the sea. Church Haven must have made a superbly sheltered anchorage although I somehow doubt it was deep enough for anything more than small coastal vessels.

Old maps of Wells make it quite clear there have been dramatic changes in the relationship between the sea and the land since the Middle Ages. The draining of the tidal basin of Church Haven after Sir John Turner built his bank was only one of them. The others included the reclamation of the area between North Point, about half a mile east of the town, and the present coast road.

West of what is now the Wells harbour channel, the changes were even more significant. You can still see the old sea walls that were built, at different times, to reclaim parts of the saltmarshes—which must have looked much like the saltmarshes on the other side of the channel do now. These walls intersect the fertile fields that produce heavy crops of rotated grains. As the saltmarshes were transformed, the Coke family gave the lie to Richard Nixon and others who have been fond of saying you can't make more land. They did, just as the Dutch had been doing for a long time, even then.

To the north, the Corsican pines planted by Coke on the dunes between Overy and Wells anchored the shifting sands and provided an effective seaward defence. When I first came here in the early 1960s, the pine woods had been established for more than a hundred years. But these dunes are fragile and their fragility has been demonstrated in the big storms that periodically attack this coast.

The fields behind the dunes where we walked today are vulnerable because there is a continuous battle between man and sea, and from time to time, as if to remind us of its latent potency, the sea comes smashing through the pine woods and the sea wall and temporarily takes back the fields that were so painfully reclaimed over a period of two hundred years.

I vividly remember that in the winter of 1953 I was at home sick with measles or some other childhood illness, when gale-force winds and January tides caused flooding up and down the east coast. I recall too the names of places of which I had never heard before and have not for the most part heard since: Canvey Island, Mablethorpe, Clacton, Skegness, Sea Palling—only the last in Norfolk and well to the east of the Magic Kingdom. There must have been some other Norfolk places too, but I don't remember them. What I do remember is the flow of gifts from the rest of Britain and from other countries to the victims of the flood. So does Glynis, who was not a victim at all but was none the less on the receiving end of such things as coffee sent from Ethiopia!

That night—31st January 1953—the sea was untamed. And those who had doubted it had ever flowed into Church Haven saw—briefly, because it did not stay long—how things used to be before Turner built his bank. I don't think Glynis, then at Wells Primary School, was one of the registered doubters. In fact, I am pretty sure that at the time she knew little or nothing of local history. But that evening, after tea with her grandparents in Church Street, she was one of those who stood at the top of the Polka (Polka Road) and saw the sea had flooded Ramm's Marsh, had flooded part of the churchyard, had flooded the railway station, and had flooded the area where the Wells Industrial Estate is now. She was unable to get home that night. Nobody died in Wells, although many animals and birds were drowned. But there were casualties all along the coast.

Magical things happened too. Wiveton found itself, once more, beside the sea. Cley, for an instant, looked like a port again. Those who did not believe the sea once ran through Holkham Gap and into what is now the lake in Holkham Park became believers; there it was. As if Rip Van Winkle had rearranged the boundaries of land and sea, familiar places became unrecognizable, dry places became wetlands, and the best way to get from some places to some other places was by boat. It is easy now to make light of that night. But it was frightening for many. Terrifying for some.

When I first came here in the 1960s I sometimes asked—in what I hoped was a proper tone of voice for a foreigner—whether the cracks in the wall that then separated the Wells harbour channel from Coke's reclaimed fields to the west were dangerous. Since I knew nothing about civil engineering, the question was innocent. Obviously the engineers and planners thought they knew the answer, because the cracks remained, year after year. Until one night in February 1978, when we were living in Bogota, the bank broke—in two places—and the fields to the west were flooded. Our friend, Richard Cracknell, decided—to hell with the fact that it was the middle of winter—that this might be a unique chance for a unique experience. So he hauled his Sharpie *Miranda* out of its winter hibernation and sailed it *over* the fields all the way to Holkham, the pine woods on his *starboard* side as he sailed west. The sea wall was soon rebuilt, as always in such circumstances, more strongly than before.

Conventional wisdom says it could never happen again. But suppose we have not yet had the one-hundred-year storm? Or the one-thousand-year storm? My own feeling is that taking the sea for granted is what Cameron would call 'a no-brainer'. It has a habit of unpredictably reclaiming, with neither grace nor finesse—what was once its domain. Most of the time, of course, the sea keeps its man-appointed rather than its own-appointed limits.

Perhaps it is apt that the price of creating more land was the death of maritime trade for most of the North Norfolk ports. Point and counterpoint; seaborne trade versus grazing and farming; saltmarshes versus freshwater marshes; sea versus man. There is an element of the elemental in the knowledge that the high tides that magically cover the marshes on summer evenings are the same tides that, earlier in the year backed by north-east gales, tighten the stomach and jog anxious memories of destruction.

The Holkham Estate still dominates North Norfolk agriculture and dwarfs all other properties. Few of the estate farms have been sold or separated. And the Estate Farm and some of the tenant farms—as results at the annual ritual of the Royal Norfolk Show confirm—measure well against the best in the county and beyond.

The major forces of change in the economy of the Magic Kingdom today have more to do with politics than with technology. After several decades of relatively high guaranteed prices, uncertainty now grips the farming community as it waits to learn the implications of Maastricht and how European Union regulations will be interpreted. How much of their arable land will have to lie fallow? Will it be the same piece of land year after year, or just the same proportion of total acreage? Can it be used for other things; houses, for example? And what will happen to the landscape? In recent years, the familiar brown, gold and green tones of our fields have been jarred by the incursion of the vivid yellow oilseed rape; 'not a proper colour for England' somebody once told me, 'belongs to the tropics' (where she had obviously never been because I've seen a lot of tropical fields and nothing compares with oilseed rape for brightness). Will the fallow fields grow weeds? Will farmers be obliged to keep up their appearances?

While there are always risks it could again break its banks, the sea, for now, is where the visionaries of the eighteenth century thought it should be. And the water that flows between the historical reclaimed fields of the Holkham Estate is fresh. But wouldn't it be ironic if, after all the effort and expense of creating them, these fields were obliged to lie fallow? Because a grey man in Brussels decided they should?

5 August

After breakfast, Glynis and I are going to look at Langham Hall again. I saw it with Cameron last Saturday. I am definitely intrigued because it is a lovely house with lots of space and a beautifully converted stable and coach-house block. Also—because it is a listed building—it belongs to the man-made part of what seems to be known these days as English Heritage and thus part of what makes the Magic Kingdom magical.

I must say, though, I am wondering more and more about how long the magic will last. I sense it could be destroyed, the main risk being too many people. How many more can it stand? Is it more fragile than I had thought? If we are approaching some kind of limit, how should the trade-off between public access and environmental protection be managed? Who should manage it? Is it a question of limits to growth or limits to freedom? Or both? I am troubled by these questions. I don't like them. They make me uncomfortable and I wish they would go away. Alas, I am sure they won't. Indeed, the fact that most things around here have, thus far, been preserved is no guarantee they will continue to be preserved. The combined forces dedicated to conservation could be overwhelmed by market forces that can be curbed and checked but only partially controlled.

The first place I ever loved was Dorset. I went there, in the spring of 1952, on what was called a 'School Journey'. Don't ask why it was called a 'School Journey'; I don't know. But it was a transformational experience that opened my eyes to a world of natural wonders: St Aldhem's Head, Durdle Door, Lulworth Cove, Poole Harbour, the Chesil Beach. And of man-made wonders: Corfe Castle, Maiden Castle. Place names that in themselves were magical: Langston Matravers, Blandford Forum, Sturminster Newton. No wonder Hardy found it hard to improve on them. And everywhere, Purbeck marble and Portland stone.

Later, when I was at school, I went back to Dorset on my bicycle three or four times, and the wonder and the mystery and the happy marriage of art and local materials was intact. My last bicycle holiday in Dorset was probably in 1956 or 1957.

Fifteen years later, living in Wimbledon, working at the International Coffee Organization in London and having long since fallen in love with both Glynis and North Norfolk, I wanted to show my wife why I still had a soft spot for Dorset. So we went back for a weekend, staying at Lulworth. The natural wonders were still there. But they had been overrun by people. And of necessity, the people had been organized: 'No Parking' here; 'No Stopping' there; 'Stay Away ' from this; 'Keep Off' that. The mysterious places were still there but they had also been overrun. And despite what I'm sure were the best and most sincere efforts of people who cared intensely about preservation and conservation, the harmony of art and stone had been assaulted by bricks, slates and other foreign materials.

The best metaphor was actually en route *to Dorset at Stonehenge, which, when I first went there (in 1956 I should think), was a lonely and lovely place. It looked, I imagined, just as it must have done when Tess—I was just beginning to read Hardy at that time—was there. Not a barrier in sight. Not a trash can to be seen. Now it was crawling with people. You couldn't get near it, much less touch it, and it might as well have been part of an American theme park or an open-air museum.*

Dorset, for me, was finished and yet another once Magic Kingdom was no longer magic. Not because anybody had set out to destroy it; they hadn't. Not because people didn't care about it; they did. But because it had collapsed under the impact of too many people applying too much pressure.

The wind is still blowing hard from the same direction. Actually, even harder than yesterday. That means we shall not sail today either and we may even have to reconsider our idea of taking John Bean's ferry from Morston to the Point and walking down the beach to Cley and from there back to Blakeney. On the other hand, the wind would be at our backs all the way.

Getting There

Although the place was beautiful, we were horrified. Not because it was raining. Or because the temperature was similar to what we later found was normal for midsummer in the Orkneys. But because there were signs all over the place saying there was no access to the beach. We eventually learned that Maine was one of only two states in the Union that allows people to own bits of beach and thus to prevent other people from getting to it. From the landward side. Along the beach from adjoining properties. Or from the sea. Let alone using it.

That just seemed all wrong to me because I had always thought beaches could not, and should not, be privately owned. Not below the highwater line anyway. Everywhere I had been before, beaches had been accessible: in Europe, the Caribbean, Africa, South and Central America, and the Middle East. Now I think back on it there must have been privately owned beaches in many of the countries I had visited. After all, most of them were not property-owning democracies. But I had certainly not run into this problem before.

The language of the signs was neither polite nor even mildly ambiguous. This was, after all, the USA where people owned guns and meant what they said. 'Keep out' meant: 'Don't Even Think of Coming Through Here'. Thanks to the unbelievably powerful National Rifle Association, the spirit of the frontier remains alive in the USA and the citizen's constitutionally decreed right to bear arms remains intact. The USA clearly is a property-owning democracy. It is also a gun-owning democracy.

Some of the time, the right to bear arms is actually presented as a God-given right, but then extremist organizations in the United States have a habit of claiming Higher Authority is on their side. I remember when Coach Joe Gibbs (of the Washington Redskins) appeared at a press conference after winning Super Bowl XIII (I don't know why they use Roman numerals; maybe it looks better), and proceeded to thank everybody for their help, including God ... 'especially God'. And then the other day, President Bush chastised Bill Clinton for having left a three letter word out of his acceptance speech at the Democratic Convention a few weeks ago; what was it? G O D. I think it follows that if Jesus Christ had been an American, he would naturally have been armed. Probably with a bazooka. Or maybe a sawn-off shotgun.

In the States, Glynis gives money to a group that is opposing the National Rifle Association and pressing for hand-gun control. Washington DC is the murder capital of the USA with an average of about 1.3 homicides a day. It is where all the Representatives and all the Senators live with their families. Yet the other side keeps winning. Why is that?

My suspicion is that in the United States, having a gun is rather like having a four-wheel drive vehicle, new terms for which are: 'all wheel drive', 'four by four', and 'alltrack'. Now, most Americans live in suburbs. And the need for either guns or alltracks in the suburbs of Anytown, USA, is highly questionable. They argue, of course, that law-abiding people need guns because criminals have guns, somehow overlooking the fact that criminals have guns because they can buy them over the counter with few, if any, constraints.

Anyway, the sort of people who put up signs saying things like: 'Posted. Keep Out', or 'Trespassers Will Be Terminated' (I made that one up) are obviously serious. People to be taken at their word. They might have guns. In Maine they might have big guns for shooting moose (a very unsatisfactory plural of moose), and for all we knew might routinely let fly at trespassers. And Maine has Republican congresspeople. Massachusetts would therefore be safer because everybody in Massachusetts is a liberal, which was not a good thing to be in the 1980s, and it has Democratic congresspeople. Just imagine what it would be like if Arizona had private beaches. They would probably mine them. It's a good thing Arizona is a hundred miles from the nearest coast.

In that first trip to Maine, we actually had a private beach that came with the little house we rented on the shore of Penobscot Bay. But it was very small and the point of being there was to explore. If we had taken a boat we could have tried getting to the beaches from the sea. But I'm sure there would have been notices bobbing about on buoys—boo-ees—saying things like 'No Landing' and 'We Take No Prisoners'. The ultimate irony about guns in America hit me earlier this summer when big, powerful water guns became very popular with children of all ages. In some places they were banned. Not because they were a public nuisance. But because in several incidents people who had been attacked with water guns retaliated by using real guns. Result: homicides. Diagnosed cause: intimidation. Answer: ban the water guns. There is a framed poster—from, I should think, the 1930s—in Christine and Rex Hiskey's house in Wells. It is about 'squirts', which at that time did not mean undersized boys, but what my generation called water pistols. They were banned in Wells too. But only because they were a nuisance.

In North Norfolk today, we are much better off. Water guns are on sale everywhere and, as far as I know, are banned nowhere—except, I imagine, in the schools. And within reason, we can go everywhere, without let or hindrance. Beaches are public property and if you want, you can walk unhindered from the Wash to

Yarmouth along the foreshore, so long as you are careful about tides. Even where there are cliffs you can get to the beaches, tides permitting.

The caveat about tides is important, because the tides determine when you can and when you can't get to the beaches between Wells and Cley. And even at low tide you can't actually get across the harbour channel at Blakeney although you can cross the channels at Overy, Wells, and Morston. A tide table, old clothes, and — depending on the time of year—waders are all you need to reach the beach across the marshes. There are several routes. The easiest one is at Stiffkey, where a series of seven wooden bridges, the outermost ones now spanning creeks filled with sand, takes you to the foreshore. There are three other tracks between there and Wells. All of them cross creeks that are full of water at high tide. Some have bridges over them. Many do not, which means you have to slip and slide your way across the mud. It is not primeval mud (which is a pity because 'primeval' is a good word), because the marshes were not there even a thousand years ago. Indeed, it is obvious, even to a casual observer—an American would say 'quite casual' and mean the same thing—that the marshes are evolving all the time.

In fact they are literally being created all the time. As the offshore spits and bars shift, protected environments are created behind them, and the sand becomes a mixture of sand and mud, and in due course all mud. Then vegetation appears and creeks form as the marsh gets deeper. Over the last decade, there has been a textbook demonstration of this process in Holkham Gap. If we go back to the 1960s, Holkham Gap was a sandy beach. By the late 1970s, a hummock of sand began to develop in the middle of the Gap. More hummocks appeared in the 1980s. Eventually, they virtually closed it. Now there is mud everywhere. And saltmarsh vegetation is developing. Another decade and the transformation will make the place unrecognizable to someone who was last there in the 1960s.

Much the same thing has happened at the western end of what is usually thought of as Wells beach. The hummocks are now twenty feet high. And the westernmost beach huts look across a broad stretch of mud; thirty years ago they surveyed the sands.

There is no obvious reason to think there is excessive pressure on Wells beach. It gets full up a few times a year, when sun and tide and school holidays coincide to draw people there from inland places. But not much more so now than in the 1960s, when at Whitsuntide one year I got sunsick for the second time in my life. It's funny, but despite having been in many countries where the sun is a lot stronger than it is in England, I've never been sunsick anywhere else. In fact the only other place it happened was

Bexhill, Sussex, when I was still at school.

The places that worry me and, I am sure, many others, are the marshes. The marshes, as I've said before, *define* the Magic Kingdom. Without them, it would not be what it is. I have always thought they were pretty much self-protecting because most people, not altogether irrationally, fear them. What do they fear? Being cut off by the tide for one thing. Getting lost by wandering out over the foreshore and not being able to find the way back afterwards. Sudden mists, which can and do roll in from the sea, although they are rarely thick. I suppose some people fear getting muddy too. Or perhaps getting stuck in the mud and sinking into it.

The former fear is, in my view, strange. After all, doesn't getting muddy somehow liberate us as adults? Those who understand exactly what I mean by that question will I suspect, agree that it does. Those who do not understand will wonder why I ask. The latter fear is, however, irrational, because Norfolk marsh mud does not suck people into it.

But with one thing and another, the marshes have always seemed able, as it were, to take care of themselves. I know a lot of people who have lived in the Magic Kingdom all their lives and have *never* been on the marshes. They may have walked along the greens that back them but the sense that they are dangerous has kept them off.

In the past, I have had two reactions. First, that it was a good thing. Not because it meant the environment was protected, but because the few who went there could continue to enjoy them in near solitude. Neither ecologically nor socially attractive but, at least in my case, true. Second, sadness that so many people were, in effect, denying themselves the best of what the Magic Kingdom had to offer.

Now, I have a third perspective. That the number of people who go on the marshes has increased in recent years. Not a lot, but enough to raise the question in my mind of where, if this should turn out to be the start of a trend, it will lead us. The faint paths that cross the saltmarsh vegetation have not, so far, had to take a lot of traffic. Let's suppose, in the course of a year—counting the hunters as well as the ornithologists and the botanists—an average of five people a day walk across a track such as that which leads to the foreshore from the bottom of the unmade road that runs down from Warham beyond the coast road. That's about 1,500 people a year. Suppose it were ten times as many?

The result, I suspect, would be that the track would get trodden in more deeply, the banks of the creeks where people scramble up and down would be degraded, and the vegetation would diminish. I'm no expert on this topic and I'm sure there are other people who have calculated the carrying capacity of the marshes (what I would call the supply side), and the probable growth in the number of people using them (the demand side). At some point, assuming more and more people have leisure time they want to spend in places like the Magic Kingdom—including physically active retirees—enough will be enough. What then?

It is, of course, wonderful that the whole of this coastline is classified as an area of outstanding natural beauty, variously managed by the Norfolk Naturalists Trust, the RSPB, English Nature, and the National Trust. Between them they have the enviable task of caring for this unique environment. But not an easy one, because they will have to make decisions about access that will please some, infuriate others, and will be deliberately ignored by many, who feel they have a right to go where they please. How will they enforce controls? It is one thing for a warden to nip across to the East Hills from Wells beach before the tide flows to make sure nobody without a boat is still there and that they have no plans to spend the night. There is a real danger of fire over there.

I accept that the freedom to camp on the East Hills had to go. I shall have a much harder time—to the point of uncivil disobedience if need be—in accepting the notion I cannot go on the marshes or, for that matter, the beaches beyond them. Perhaps there is room for compromise. Rationing would be one option. Perhaps everyone might be allowed on the marshes for a limited number of days per year. It could be an honour system which would depend on self-regulation. Or it could be controlled by full-time officials—volunteers perhaps—who would stamp your ration book. They use a similar system to regulate the number of cars in Mexico City. It would have nasty totalitarian overtones. Would it work? As Cameron might say: *Not!*

Another option might be to use the most primitive allocative system known to economics: the queue. Set up turnstiles at the ends of the unmade roads that provide access to the marshes from the coast road and control the flow of people. Would that work better? Again: *Not!*

I think the dilemma over what to do about access is only beginning to emerge in many people's minds. Certainly in mine. For thirty years my family and I have been free to wander at will in this lonely and lovely wonderland, rarely meeting another person. But, just the other day, I was at first alarmed, then angry, then perplexed, when I heard of a proposal to ban access to the marshes. I was furious that somebody might want to constrain my freedom and prevent me, and others, from continuing to wander—respectfully and carefully—at will. I hate this dilemma; and a dilemma it is, since dilemmas are problems that don't have solutions.

I have always thought it was a good idea not to signpost the unmade roads that lead to the marshes. And I still think so. Being a pragmatist, I am happy to play for time, putting off the truly evil day when people will be told there is no access. We should use it to find a creative solution that would not impose more constraints than are essential for environmental protection. This is, after all, a sophisticated country and people here have an intuitive sense of what is right and wrong when it comes to land use. I wish I had something in mind. I don't. But my experience in public policy making tells me there has to be a better way than either of two solutions that come to mind.

First example. When we lived in the Dominican Republic in the 1960s, forest degradation was a serious and urgent problem, mainly because a growing rural population was making excessive use of the remaining forests to make charcoal, their primary cooking fuel. Solution: put the forests under the control of the Army. Effective, but crude in the extreme.

Second example. The environment of Yellowstone National Park in Wyoming is extremely fragile and very precious, particularly the areas around the hot springs. The park gets more than a million visitors a year, most of them over a rather brief period in the summer because in the long, cold, and snowbound winter the park is inaccessible to all but the ultra hardy with 'alltrack' vehicles. When the crowds are there, apart from the need to separate people from scalding water (which might, after all, put people off), you also have to keep them off the congealed lava from which steam hisses and hot water burbles because, if trampled on by a million feet a year, it would soon be ruined. So you confine the visitors to boardwalks. It is all done about as well as one imagines it could be done. And the physical constraints are obviously necessary. But what would Warham marshes look like with a boardwalk? I hope I shall never see one. But I fear that my unborn grandchildren may grow up knowing nothing else.

7 August

As it turned out, we did not go to the Point yesterday. We went to Norwich. To buy a few things we really needed like small plates to complement our other stoneware, a book for Glynis from the university bookshop at Earlham, and a copy of A Year in Provence *(which Glynis says I should read while I am writing this). And a few things we did not need but wanted, like a compact disc by an Irish group called Clannad which was highly praised in a review in the* Washington Post *a few weeks ago but is not actually on sale in the States yet. And some food for the supper party we are having tomorrow, although perhaps that falls under 'needs'. We also got some things we might otherwise have bought in Fakenham, but chose to get in Norwich instead.*

Buying things here—from soap to nuts—is very different from buying things in the USA. It's not just a matter of using different words for the same things, or using different money to buy them. The things themselves are different too. As are the attitudes of the people who sell them. A myriad of other things—little things—all in themselves rather trivial that make up the warp and the woof of daily life, are also different. The newspapers are different. The television is different. And the details are different. I used to work with somebody who kept telling me 'the devil is in the details'. Well, maybe so and maybe not. But when I think about it, the difference is certainly in the details.

Little Things

One of the many pleasures of travel—I think the greatest one—is getting a feel for what life is like for people who live in other places. The most obvious way to do that is to meet people. Talk to them. Visit their homes. Meet their spouses and children. And do with them at weekends whatever it is they do at weekends. Play tennis at a country club. Enjoy the beach. Walk. Listen to music. Go to the theatre. The possibilities are endless.

Meeting people in their offices during working hours tells you very little about them. Meeting them with their families gives you a much better sense of who they really are. Official relationships become personal relationships. Communications improve. Trust is enhanced.

Listening to local radio and watching local television gives you another set of impressions. In some places, local radio not only tells you about dialect, diction,and accent. It also tells you about local things: local issues, local priorities, local values. It gives you a level of detail that is unusually vivid and authentic.

I remember, for example, a few years ago, driving from Rugby (where I had been to see Caitlin) to Cambridge (where I was going to see Carey), listening to a programme on Radio Northamptonshire about a place called Higham Ferrers. It was a sort of radio documentary, in which the reporter went from one location to another in the village (or maybe it's a town) of Higham Ferrers, talking to people and describing what he saw. I had never visited Higham Ferrers, I knew nothing about it, and I'm pretty sure that, half an hour earlier, I didn't even know it existed. Yet in a quiet and subtle way, it was quite gripping.

Now I was, of course, sitting in a car. I had the option of finding another radio station. But I was, in a sense, part of a captive mobile audience because I was not going to get out until I reached Cambridge. I am fairly certain I would not have listened to it at home. But being where I was, I listened willingly. Not because I needed information about Higham Ferrers or knew what to do with the information once I had it. But because it was like having a very-large-scale map brought to life. Although I could see neither the place nor the people, through the eye of my mind, and with the help of my ear, I got a visual impression of them.

That sort of insight is a bit like the insight you get from walking; the slower you go, the more detailed the impression. You therefore get more from walking than from jogging. More from jogging than from cycling. More from cycling than from driving. And much more from driving than from flying, from which you get nothing at all.

An aircraft is, in effect, a space capsule. You get in at one place and get out at another, and all there is in between is the air through which you fly. From time to time, if the air is clear, you can see the ground.

But in a commercial jet at thirty-five thousand feet, things on the ground look very small and there are no details. The only thing remotely like it is looking at the landscape from the top of a mountain, and seeing the world in a new perspective.

The polar ice caps are very beautiful from the warm cabin of a 747. The grandeur, immensity, and loneliness of the Andes between Peru and Argentina are overwhelming. And the vast scale and sheer monotony of the Plains states as you fly across enormous spreads of grain are unforgettable. I have sometimes wondered about the impressions of the Magic Kingdom picked up from the air by the crews of the F-111s, A-10s, and Tornadoes from Sculthorpe and elsewhere as they practise bombing runs from what looks (and sounds) like one thousand feet on summer afternoons over the sea. I have always imagined it must be a blur. Now, stopping to think more carefully, I suppose they are looking at their instruments rather than out of their windows. That means they have no impression at all.

There is a peculiar phenomenon that, in my experience, mostly occurs on trains. You are sitting in a train, watching the world roll by. And suddenly—the whole thing lasts for perhaps twenty seconds—in the near but not too near distance, you see a composition: a woman hanging out washing in her back garden, she looks up as the train passes but carries on hanging...; a village cricket match, some of the players are not wearing whites, a medium-pace bowler turns for his run, a boy is adjusting the scoreboard of numbered plates hanging on hooks (which takes a minute or two so the scoreboard is never accurate until they stop for tea or someone is out)...; Sussex, the translucent light of early evening, a five-barred gate into a field by a tall oak tree, three children—two with bicycles—looking up as the train hisses by...; moments in time, almost still-life pictures. And they stay in your memory for twenty, thirty, forty, years. Those pictures were all taken from steam trains...

Less often than on trains—at least, in my experience—the same phenomenon happens on buses although never in cars. The bus must be old. From the front, the radiator, bonnet (hood),and windshield must convey an idea of its character: smooth, craggy, grouchy, mean, supercilious. They don't make buses like that any more. So the bus is old. And noisy. And slow.

Glynis and I are spending part of the summer of 1962 working in Alf Dunthorne's field labour gang that he hires out to farmers who need seasonal help with things like stringing beans, strawing strawberries, and hoeing carrots. Early morning. Between Wells and Walsingham, going through Wighton. Sharp left turn as you come into the village; on the grass at the roadside, an old man; ancient and battered hat, collarless shirt, laces round his trousers below the knee. He must be long since gone. And he wouldn't remember anyway because he sat there every day for a few hours, watching the then occasional car or bus go by. There is now so much more traffic that if he were still there, he would be headless from having yanked his head from side to side, like a spectator at the Centre Court.

Television is intrinsically less local than what used to be called—I've never known why—steam radio. Particularly now that we have CNN in hotel rooms around the world. Today, you can watch a broadcast originating in Atlanta, Georgia, not only in homes and hotels throughout the USA, but also in the Intercontinental in Kinshasa, the Hilton in Jerusalem, and the Inn on the Park in London. Television distorts the reality of spatial separation by seeming to eliminate it; one world, one moment in time, one data base.

In North Norfolk, television also distorts reality by trying to make us believe we are actually living in Yorkshire. There's nothing wrong with Yorkshire (or certain bits of it, anyway). But most of us are puzzled—and a bit put-out—by the fact that North Norfolk receives Yorkshire Television but not Anglia, and the BBC enables us to watch 'Look North' but not 'Look East'. There is an answer to the puzzle: an interesting one. The Cromer Ridge, which is the terminal moraine of a glacier of the last Ice Age, has a powerful effect on television signals from the south. It is impossible to get good transmission of Anglia television programmes, but there is no problem in beaming down signals from much farther north. Due note of this is taken for commercial purposes, and viewers in Yorkshire and North Derbyshire are as puzzled by advertisements for garages and shops in King's Lynn and Great Yarmouth as those in North Norfolk are by advertisements for Derbyshire and Yorkshire.

As it happens, I am interested in what is happening in Norfolk but I don't give a hoot about what is happening in Yorkshire. I don't want to know about special offers on cars in Bingley, Batley, and Bradford; great deals on carpets in Castleford; or lowest prices ever on washing machines in Wakefield. And it's not because I lack unfulfilled ambitions to visit those places. Or because I am not usually in the market for consumer durables when I'm on holiday. It's because North Norfolk is in Norfolk and the television is trying to persuade me I'm wrong when I know damn well I'm right. I want the television to confirm I am where I think I am.

That's one of the reasons I read the *Eastern Daily Press* when we're here. Not because it's a better newspaper than the *Independent*. In my view, it's not. But because it certifies, every day, that I am where I think I am. On Martha's Vineyard, I read the splendid *Vineyard Gazette* although, since it is published twice weekly, it only confirms I am where I think I am on Tuesdays and Fridays.

Some people have local newspapers—like the *Eastern Daily Press* and the *Vineyard Gazette*—delivered to them on the other side of the world (usually a few days late, of course, since neither produces an overseas edition). That makes no sense to me. When I am in Washington I read the *Washington Post* and the *Washingtonian* magazine because they are published where I am. As it happens I also read the London *Times* and the *Independent*, but they are not really local newspapers and their coverage of world events is superior to that of the *Post*. No, I read the *EDP* avidly when I am here *because* I am here; and I do not read it when I am not here because I am not here.

The whole point of local radio, local television, and local newspapers is that—like trains with picture windows, and old buses that crawl slowly around country roads—they give you insight. They help you penetrate beneath the surface of the obvious. And, sometimes at least, help you understand what life is like wherever it is you are.

Ultimately, if you really want to understand, you must participate. The real traveller does not simply visit places; he lives in them. The accounts of nineteenth century travellers to Bogota are authentic and real because they did not go there for ten days; they went for ten months. Or a year and a half, hence Hamilton's memoir: *Eighteen Months in the Colombian Andes*.

Many self-styled travellers in our own century have done things differently. I recall that when we lived in Colombia in the 1960s, a very well-known American 'travel' writer, who had written a series of successful books about South America, swung through Bogota to 'update' his work. He stayed three days and didn't leave the capital! Since then, I've learned that a great deal of what passes for authentic reporting about other places is superficial, biased, and often just plain wrong. The problem is that in the more exotic parts of the world, they usually get away with it.

For most of us, however, the issue is not how to go about reporting on other places, but about how we, ourselves, for our own private satisfaction, can get to know and understand them. Even if the visit is brief, there are always alternatives to the homogenized, pasteurized, and sanitized hotels that are deliberately made to be (or at least to seem) identical the world over. And there are always other things—local things—to eat and drink than those that, also by design, are the same everywhere.

There are risks. Going native doesn't mean going crazy. You don't have to rush from your hotel to the nearest vendor of whatever it is they cook on the street where you are. And it pays to be careful, which means no more than using common sense. January 1979, 3.00 am, Nairobi. Not in the 'Norfolk' because it is full. The 'New Stanley' instead. I wake up, vomiting. Call the front desk. Ask for a doctor. I talk to one on the telephone. He asks me what I had for dinner. Oysters. Serves you right, he says. Lesson learned. A few years later, after I joined the Bank, a restaurant in the 'Zona Rosa' in Mexico City; it had (and I think still has) a 'vomitorium'.

Restaurants in the Magic Kingdom do not have things like that. However, eating and drinking here have become a lot more interesting in recent years. There is still only a handful of what might be described, I suppose, as 'serious' restaurants, although I always find that term a bit uppity. Where are they?

Well, there's 'Fishes' in Burnham Market, which is very good at what you would expect it to be good at; simple preparation, always fresh fish and shellfish (some, though not much of it, local); a nice sitting room where you can have an aperitif while you decide what to eat; wholesome, unpretentious (which is not necessarily true of everything in Burnham Market). And not expensive either.

Then there's the 'Moorings' in Wells just around the corner from the quay. Not the most attractive part of town. But this little restaurant has not been put off its confident stride by its location. It's been there nearly ten years now and has been extremely successful. Quite adventurous but classical and very reliable. The national as well as local press has covered it accurately and favourably. During the summer at least, it always seems to be full.

'Morston Hall' opened for business as a country house hotel in the late 1980s and has recently been through a change of ownership. Now, recession or no recession, it seems to have hit its stride. There is another country house hotel (a bit beyond the borders of the Magic Kingdom) that is as good an example of its kind as any in England. This is 'Congham Hall' in Grimston, just this side of Kings Lynn. We have only been there for special occasions but it's so good you wish there were more of them. Here, however, as elsewhere, the average life expectancy of restaurants and hotels is shorter than that of a player in the National Football League in the States. For a couple of years we had a country house hotel right next to us in Binham in what used to be Abbey Farm House. We thought it was superb. And a splendid use for a house that was obviously a bit too big for a family. It lasted two years. Interestingly, though, all the other places I've mentioned have been around for quite some time—several years at least—so I suppose there are exceptions to prove the rule. Before you go to a country house hotel, check to make sure it's still in business.

In the United States, where the bumper sticker is a legitimate art form, one of those you see most often is: 'Born To Shop'. I suspect people who put that sticker on their cars are good travellers as well as good shoppers because, in my view, shopping, as a way of getting to know places, is a very reliable source of insight. It's also a lot safer than eating and drinking. In fact, the best way to grasp the differences between where you live the rest of the time and the place you are visiting is to go shopping.

By which I don't mean buying things: I mean looking at thing, feeling them, prodding them , shaking them, trying them on, or whatever it is you do with the thing in question. The Master Shopper (sorry I can't think of a gender neutral way of saying that) hardly ever *buys* things. Triumph is returning home empty handed, having successfully demonstrated—to your own satisfaction—there was nothing worth buying. You have a sense of exhausted well-being you get after swimming the English Channel or climbing Mount McKinley. And you are not a penny poorer. In fact you may even be better off if you saved on lunch because you had to finish making your comparisons and therefore skipped it.

The biggest difference these days—by which I mean *this year*, because things can change a lot from one year to the next—between the shops in Washington and the shops in North Norfolk is that almost everything costs much more here. In most cases, and with a few exceptions, about twice as much as in Washington. The exceptions? Flowers. And plants. That's it. Everything else, this year, costs about the same in dollars as in pounds, and at current exchange rates that means double.

Some of the things you can buy are different too. Today, I ran into a man in Howells' Superstores who was complaining you couldn't buy frozen yoghourt in this country. He kept going on about how popular it is in what he called America (which is fine; sometimes I call it that too). Eventually, Kenny Howell told him I lived in America most of the time and must know all about it. But I told him I'd never eaten frozen yoghourt in my life and if that was the only difference he knew about he had missed a lot. The man seemed quite upset and slunk off muttering about yoghourt. At least, I think that's what he was muttering about. Maybe it was about me.

If frozen yoghourt were available in this country, I'm sure Howells' would have it. They have a sign outside that says: 'Stop Here. We Sell Everything'. That's not literally true, of course. But between the food shop and the adjacent hardware shop they do sell an amazing variety of stuff. Things have changed enormously since we came here. Ten years ago, who would have thought they'd now be offering not just champagne but three kinds of champagne? And four kinds of gin. And patum peperum. And exotic jams and marmalades. And all sorts of other non-traditional food and drink. The cause is obvious: the invaders (and, I have to say, at least in this context, that means us as well as the burpies) have brought their tastes with them. And as long as their money is good, Trevor and Kenny will sell them whatever they want. In the last three weeks I've bought from them, among other things, an inner tube for Catriona's bicycle, a staw boater, several plastic model aircraft for Cameron, dandelion wine, candles, a whoopee cushion, a wood rasp, rhubarb and ginger jam, and home-made fruit bread that comes only on Tuesdays and is sold out by ten o'clock.

They don't make shops and stores like that in the States any more although there are a few that have been tenderly preserved, as though they were museums. There's one called Alley's almost in the middle of Martha's Vineyard, in the village of West Tisbury. It is revered as a piece of real Americana and is visited by people who don't really need to buy anything but none the less make the pilgrimage to this shrine-like emporium. It's probably on the National Registry of Historic Places. If not, it will be. It's a working store. But its stock is quite limited. And it's self-conscious, a bit precious. Nobody is likely to slap a conservation order on Howells' Superstores. But Alley's typifies the shops that Americans would like to remember from childhoods they did not have, in small towns and villages with maple-shaded streets they would like to have come from, but didn't, because they were not there. It's the sort of shop a set designer would produce for a film about life on the western frontier in the early nineteenth century. Norman Rockwell would have loved it.

My favourite shops aren't actually shops at all. They are known as chandleries. In my opinion, the English do them better than the Americans. There are three here: at Wells, Overy Staithe, and Blakeney. And they are all the real thing, meaning they sell the things that chandleries are supposed to sell and don't go in for beach toys and buckets and spades and other kinds of seaside paraphernalia.

Beams are essential to a proper chandlery. Things have to hang from them, often so low you have to navigate carefully around them, new views opening as you weave your way through obstacle courses of folding anchors and strings of galvanized shackles—though most of them, these days (the shackles, that is), seem to be made of stainless steel. Chandleries must also have the right smell. In the States I think there would be a good market for aerosol cans of authentic chandlery odours. After all, in McLean, Virginia, I recently saw some small cans of 'new leather' perfume to preserve that 'just new' smell. If that, why not a delicate potpourri of selected marine pongs?

Of course, chandleries these days don't smell primarily of leather. Not a very nautical material any more, except in boatshoes. Some of them still smell of rope, although synthetics are putting an end to that. And varnish. And oil. And new wool. I particularly like the chandlery in Blakeney, Stratton Long Marine, which has wonderful wool sweaters that replicate patterns traditionally worn by local fishermen. At one time, every town and village along the coast had its own. Unfortunately, the only ones now being made commercially are from Cromer and Sheringham. The Wells pattern was rediscovered a few years ago and my mother-in-law made me one from the old instructions.

So now I have all three, two of them from places outside the Magic Kingdom. It's funny. Back in the States, I find my perspective shifts just enough so that I can wear all of them without fretting about their exact origins. But then distance makes the heart grow fonder. Right?

9 August

The weather has broken and I am back to an odious habit: calling the weatherline to find out if it is going to rain. As if they knew anyway! Today looks fine at the moment, but the weatherline says there will be showers this afternoon. So if we're going to do something outside, we'd better start this morning. Only five more days until we leave.

Tomorrow we'll be getting ready for another supper party. The last one went off very well, especially Glynis's crème brulée. It's odd to think of it now, but in the past we have always taken short cuts to entertaining, often buying ready prepared food at Humble Pie in Burnham Market and Picnic Fare in Cley. Looking back (this is the first time we've thought it odd), it seems incredible that we—the ones on holiday—didn't have time to do things properly without short cuts. Whereas our guests have always been working at whatever it is they do: farming, photography, building, soliciting (the kind solicitors do), insurance, looking after Blickling Hall, writing, teaching, boatbuilding, acting, retailing, running a hotel, and so on and so forth. Yet when they have hosted us, they've always come up with amazing food and wine over which they have taken a lot of time and effort, despite the fact they've had jobs to do as well.

We've always told each other it was because our house was not properly equipped for cooking: not enough special pots and pans and other things we have back at the ranch in McLean. But that's a feeble excuse because what we have here is essentially what we used to have in London and we managed there all right. Anyway, this year we have decided we'll make more effort to do things ourselves and have fun doing it.

'Of course', Glynis has said from time to time, 'they all have Agas'. To the uninitiated, I should explain that the Aga cooker is as much a part of life among our friends here as the French car and the wooden boat. They are all icons. My suspicion is that the Aga symbolizes Mother Country. I might have said Mother Norfolk, but I have a sense that Agas are ubiquitous in rural England and are not peculiar to Norfolk. I dare say, in fact, that the Aga is the centre of the household in country houses (not to be confused with Country Houses) in Somerset and Cumbria too.

I'm sure I'm missing something but I have a feeling it's all a bit overdone. I also have the impression it takes about five years and a couple of Cordon Bleu courses to learn how to boil eggs on an Aga. So even if we had one, we would never get enough practice on our holidays to be able to knock off the roasts and the pies and the other wonderful things we eat at our friends' houses.

I had better stop writing soon and consult with my family about what we are going to do today. There are still quite a lot of places we have not been to, even though this is my fourth week and Glynis's eighth. My tide watch—an indispensable device, I tell myself, but I know damn well it's only a toy and so does everybody else—tells me it's getting on for low water in Wells. So perhaps we'll go across the marshes from Warham to the East Hills, and then down the Wells harbour channel to the quay and back to Warham. That's one thing we always do that I would not want to miss, because it penetrates the very heart of the Magic Kingdom.

A Pilgrimage

We got back just before it started to rain and now the rain is bouncing off the tiles and velux roof lights above my head. Wonderful walk. Always is. Perhaps the best of all.

As we drove through Warham we passed the White House which, when the Dyballs lived there in the 1960s, was the second 'country house' I was ever in. As we got to the coast road, I noticed that 'they' (in this instance the Norfolk County Council) had removed the sign at the end of the unmade road that leads from there to the marshes.

I first spotted that notice a couple of years ago (Americans would say 'couple years'; I can't think why they leave out the preposition) because I tend to notice signs that say things like: 'Unsuitable for Motors'. Now it's perfectly true that this unmade road *is* unsuitable for motors if you want to bomb along it at fifty miles an hour, leaving chunks of your car on the ground on the way. But if you simply want to get to the marshes, there is no reason to go faster than, say, ten or fifteen miles an hour. And at that speed, the going is perfectly acceptable. Actually a damn sight better than most of the roads I've driven on outside the US and Europe.

I was glad the sign has gone. First, because it hinted at restricted access to what is, as far as I'm concerned, the centre of the known universe. I admit to being paranoic about that; after all, the fact you're paranoid doesn't mean you're not being followed, does it? Second, it gave me no choice than deliberately to ignore the authority of the County Council (the Norfolk equivalent of the old Supreme Soviet) and, for reasons I'd rather not explore, I've always been reluctant to ignore authority. I've usually explained that to myself (and when essential, others) as a function of my nationality. Somehow, I don't think that's the real answer, but it will do for now.

Anyway, the sign has gone but when we got to the end of the unmade road we found that 'they' had been busy down there too. The opening gambit (as I think they say in chess) was to dissuade people from going to the marshes at all by discouraging them from driving down the unmade road. The next ploy (is that also a chess word, I wonder?) was to put a heavy metal gate at the end of it with a large iron padlock on it. That means you can no longer park on Warham Greens at the edge of the marshes.

Actually, I'm rather in favour of that. Of course, I'm well aware it makes no difference whether I support this initiative or oppose it, but it's not a bad idea. Not that there were ever many cars there. But it denies access—from here at least—to people who want to get on the greens so they can drive along them towards Stiffkey or Wells. Farther east, there is access at both Stiffkey and Morston and on a given afternoon you may meet as many as a dozen cars being mindlessly driven from east to west or west to east. Some years ago, people were taking motorized 'dirt bikes' down there that made a noise like a rookery in overdrive, but that seems to have been a short-lived fad. Just as well.

As we set out across the marsh, Cameron ran ahead over the broken and now very partial remains of the wood and iron tracks that were laid in the war. The bridge over the biggest creek has been repaired since we were last here, in fact rebuilt, in an appropriately rough way. The tides have been low the last few days and it has not rained much, so the salt-smeared path that marks the way was fairly dry.

I caught up with Cameron. 'This', I said, 'is a very special place. In fact, the most special place in the world to me.' No response. 'So, what do you think of it?'

'It's all right', he said.

I didn't push it, sensing that it was a pretty dumb question to ask a ten-year-old boy. Especially taking account of the fact that its most striking feature is its flatness.

To the north east, as we reached the seaward side of the marsh and came on to the sand that is covered twice a day by the tide, was the bump of Blakeney Point, and the square grey box of the old lifeboat house on its landward side. To the north west, the way we began to walk, were the dunes and stunted pines of the East Hills. And between them, to the north, the sand sloped gently over more than a mile to the invisible sea. Behind us now at ground level, the sea lavender was fading, its brilliant July plumage turning silver in the shrinking days.

I again thought of winter, when the ground is hard and there is ice in the tidal pools on top of the marsh and, where we walked today, there are duck and geese. We shall be back in America long before they return. It's odd how seasons mean more as you get older. I remember being at a seminar in Hungary soon after we were married in 1964 and hearing the wife of an American college professor explain how the seasons had come to mean more to her as she had grown older. I really didn't understand what she talking about. That was before we had lived in the tropics, and before each season had come to bring its own peculiar joys and celebrations that measure the music of time.

Cameron eventually told me, as we walked on, getting closer to the Hills, that he supposed it was a pretty neat place. In the American sense of course: nothing to do with tidy. More like 'attractive' in English English. Of all our children, Cameron is by far the most American. I don't think that's because he was the only one of the four born there—Carey having been born in Santo Domingo, Caitlin in London, and Catriona in Bogota. After all, they all grew up there and even went to the same schools until first Carey, and then Caitlin, came to Rugby for the last two years. But he is certainly less intrigued by what are (to him) foreign places than his sisters.

Last year, after three weeks exploring south and south west Mexico, we spent our last afternoon visiting the remains of the great Aztec city of Tehotehuacan, and as we walked down from the top of the Temple of the Sun, I asked him what he thought of it, and he said: 'It's all right. But I've had enough of this Spanish stuff. I want to go back to Virginia'. Actually, he later said something very like that this morning.

I remember quite well carrying all my children across these sands to the East Hills on my shoulders—'Up top, Daddy'—splashing through surface water in which the sky and the clouds were perfectly reproduced except where they were corrugated by rippled sand. We reached the eastern end of the Hills where the dunes degenerate into humps and undulations before merging with the flat foreshore. Further west, towards the corner of the Hills opposite the lifeboat house, where the north–south line of the Wells harbour channel meets the west–east run of the beach, the dunes are bigger—as much as thirty to forty feet, I'd guess, although I'm a very poor estimator of distances—and the trees are taller and closer together.

In that corner, there is a clearing where we have often picnicked: going up in the morning on the last of the ebb, leaving *Pocahontas* on the drying mud near the Pool buoy, walking along the beach up to the clearing, and staying there all day until the first of the flood takes us back to the sailing club slipway.

If we had been up really early this morning, or if I hadn't spent an hour or so writing, we could have done that today. But, as I now know, we'd have been drenched before there was enough water to get back on. Also, there would have been more wind than we would have wanted. Even now, it's whining through the tiles over my head and shaking the crab apple tree in the courtyard.

Instead, we made the most of the low tide. After our picnic—not in the clearing but in the dunes—we walked round the back of the Hills on a faint track that follows the edge of the marsh, past the salt-pans where we once played cricket for hours in 1962 or 1963. We didn't have a boat then, except our canoe, *Shalom*, which was not quite the thing for a family party, so an old fisherman named Finch, long since dead, put us across in the morning and came back to collect us when the tide began to flow in the afternoon.

The track peters out beyond the southernmost and smallest trees, but a bit to the left there is the beginning of another path which you would probably not notice if you were not looking for it. A thin, uneven ribbon of salt-caked mud fringed with glasswort, it seems to be going nowhere. As I always do near the point where it begins, I tensed. How long was it since we last took this path? Two years? Three? Four? Ten?

I thought of another time when we had come this way. I had thought my tide watch was set correctly, but it was wrong by two hours. And when I got to the sands opposite the quay, the tide was pouring in and it was too late to walk across. A 'visitor' on a cruiser recently unstuck from the bottom and back in its element had a dinghy at hand. He rowed me across. And he told me I should be more careful if I didn't know my way around. Never before. Never again.

Or nearly never before if I count the time when we had been to the Hills and a big tide came churning through the Pool and we cast off in *Pocahontas* as soon as there was enough water because it was getting cold and Catriona was still a small baby. I had sailed up in the morning with Carey and Caitlin, and Glynis had come in the car, leaving it in the beach parking area on the other side of the channel. So I set her down on a sandbank on the other side, south of the lifeboat house, forgetting there was water beyond the sandbank that she'd have to cross. She did; wading up to her chest with Catriona high above her head as the rest of us watched in horror, unable to get back to her because the tide was too strong. Local knowledge indeed!

Today, all was well. The tide was still slack and we had a couple of hours to spare when we reached the tidal pool we call the 'Hot Boiler'—where Glynis learned to swim—opposite what used to be the Shipwrights Arms. As we crossed the channel where, twenty years ago, there were mussel lays, but now only sand, the water was no more than ankle deep.

We walked back to Warham Greens along the new (fifteen years is still new, I think) coast defence bank, the latest in the long line of barriers erected to keep the sea out since Sir John Turner built his bank in the eighteenth century, to North Point. And then on the broad, grassy path beside fields where sugar beet was still growing and wheat and barley were growing a fortnight ago, to the end of the unmade road that is called Cockleshell Drove on some maps.

It began to rain as we drove slowly along it up to the coast road and we told ourselves we'd been very clever to arrange things like that. Of course, we were just lucky. But it was a good pilgrimage. And Cameron will learn to love it. Eventually.

10 August

Two nights ago, we went to have dinner at an amazing place called the Saracen's Head at Wolterton. I found it in the Good Pubs Guide. It was an excellent recommendation, and I have now concluded, having been a loyal follower of Mr Ronay for many years, that this guide is probably better than his. Actually, I often use two or three guides, cross-checking them to test for consistency, but that mainly applies to hotels and restaurants rather than pubs.

The Saracen's Head is an extraordinary Georgian building of three stories with very large overhangs. Two tiny bars and a pretty dining room that we had to ourselves. I'm always thrilled to discover fine food in an out-of-the-way place that nobody has ever heard of. And Wolterton is really *out of the way. Here, for example, we had a choice of things like hare in marsala sauce, escalope of turkey in Pernod and cream, and apricot-stuffed leg of lamb en croute. A real find. But I found something else too. Temptation.*

It struck me as we drove there that the countryside between Holt and Wolterton was remarkably unspoiled. I really don't trust my memory of these things, but it seemed to me it was a bit like the Magic Kingdom used to be thirty years ago: very narrow roads without passing places, so that if you met someone coming the other way, one of you had to back up. Grass growing in the middle of some of them. Few new buildings of any sort. No traffic to speak of. And tiny villages that make Binham look like a small town.

And I thought: this is *an attractive place. One I had driven through before on the way to somewhere else but had somehow never noticed.*

Was this a case of 'some enchanted evening'? I recall that Peter Beck at the Overy Boathouse once built a whole series of OK dinghies and named them all after melodies from South Pacific, *one of them* Some Enchanted Evening. *I was so enchanted in fact that the next morning I found myself asking the estate agents in Holt about properties in the area. No harm in asking, I told myself. I'm only curious.*

All day yesterday, I was unable to get the place out of my mind and I realized, with a mixture of surprise and horror, that I was infatuated. It was not the fault of the place. After all, it had made no kind of overture to me; it was the other way round. From the settlement pattern on the map, which I had also looked at many times before but only for the purpose of finding my way, I tried to define it. There is no coastline, because it is south of Cromer and Sheringham. And it is roughly bounded by the A140 to the east, the B1149 to the west, and the B1354 to the south. I had—as though for the very first time—met this place casually one fine summer evening. It had employed no guile yet there I was, like a lovesick Larry, in thrall to its transparent innocence, freshness and naïvety.

That was yesterday. Today, even though I am fully aware of what's happening, I still don't have my feelings under control. So help me: the only thing for it is to stay west of Holt until we leave and then this silly idea will go away. What was I thinking of ? Estate agents indeed! I should be old enough to manage my feelings a bit better than that! Still, I feel a sort of magnetic compulsion to see it again. What is it like by day; a cold rainy day for example? Lots of places look fine in the translucent light of evening. But what about the next morning? Should I go there now: to see? No, I shall not. I shall impose self-discipline and control.

I think of Jimmy Carter, during the 1980 election campaign. When asked by a journalist whether he'd had extra-marital affairs, he explained he had 'lusted after women many times in his heart' but had remained faithful to Rosalind. Most people thought that was a pretty pusillanimous answer (I suppose we would now say 'wimpy'), but here I am in a similar position, determined, whatever the passing fancy, to remain loyal to the Magic Kingdom. I know I shall. But I really can't get that place with its Little Barninghams, and Plumsteads, and Edgefields out of my mind.

Balance

The other day, Glynis and I did something neither of us had done for at least thirty years: we listened to a play on the radio. It's not that I don't listen to the radio in the States. In fact I listen to it almost all the time driving to and from my office, which means for about three-quarters of an hour on an average day. And at weekends, driving around McLean and Washington. And sometimes, on long car trips, we listen to radio when we're curious about what's on people's minds up here (or down there). You learn a lot that way. But unless you count the little playlets, or mini-dramas, or whatever you'd call them, on Garrison Keillor's programme from Lake Woebegone (which is a programme about a place if ever there was one, because even though Keillor says it doesn't exist, he only means you won't find it on a map; it's there all right), I have listened to radio drama only in England, a long time ago.

By chance, however, as I was driving back from Holt yesterday morning (where I had been chatting to estate agents), I heard an announcer on Radio Four describing a play about Arthur Ransome to be broadcast at two o'clock. And I decided there was nothing I'd rather do than listen to it. To my surprise —I'll explain why later—Glynis said she'd like to listen too. So after lunch, we settled ourselves comfortably, just like we were children, not quite sure what to look at, and listened.

I understand there is a sizeable army—perhaps navy would be more appropriate, given his interests—of what might be called Ransomaniacs. They are now, like me, in their middle age and they grew up on *Swallows and Amazons*, *Secret Water*, *Coot Club*, and *Great Northern*. I was still at my primary school when I read *Coot Club* for the first time. In fact, it's the first book I remember reading. After that, I read all the others. Many times over.

As a child, I didn't have my own copies. But the public library in Kensal Rise had the hard-cover ones from Macmillan with good maps in the endpapers and lots of pen-and-ink drawings. My favourite drawing was Roger's picture of a dark night 'when it's all squishy black'; all black, in fact. I think it was reading those books that made me realize there was a world beyond Kensal Rise and Harlesden and Willesden Green. Although that world was beyond reach, I envied the children of Ransome's books. And I think it was through them that I began to understand that you could love places as well as people.

In recent years, there have been several publications about Ransome's life and work, and I am almost as intrigued by Arthur Ransome, the man, as by Arthur Ransome, the storyteller and maker-of-places-come-alive-in-print. His preface to *Swallows and*

Amazons says it all:

> as children, my brother, sisters and I spent most of our holidays on a farm at the south end of Coniston...We adored the place. Coming to it we used to run down to the lake, dip our hands. Going away from it we were half drowned in tears. While away from it, as children and as grown-ups, we dreamt about it. No matter where I was, wandering about the world, I used at night to look for the North Star and, in my mind's eye, could see the beloved skyline of great hills beneath it.

Arthur Ransome wrote about Magic Kingdoms. And he understood and captured the soul of each of them so well, one might wonder if he was something of polygamist with respect to places. But, allowing for the fact that his marital life was indeed a bit complicated, I prefer to think of him as having an unusual capacity to form loving relationships, each sincere, with a succession of places, while remaining faithful throughout his life to his first love: the Lakes.

He got around. There was a Russian period before and during the revolution of 1917 when, as the correspondent of the *Manchester Guardian*, he met Evgenia, at that time Trotsky's secretary, with whom he spent the rest of his life. But Russia was different; he did not write about its places and peoples in the way he later wrote about magic parts of Britain. There was a Scottish period when he bottled the spirit of the West Highlands in *Great Northern* and *The Picts and the Martyrs*. There was a Suffolk period when he wrote about the Orwell estuary in *Secret Water* and *We Didn't Mean to go to Sea*. And there was, of course, a Norfolk period, limited to the then (almost) pristine Broads in *Coot Club* and *The Big Six*. But his abiding passion, and the setting for most of his stories, was for the Lakes of what is now Cumbria. I should add, for those who wonder about where *Peter Duck* and *Missy Lee* fit in, that they did not fit in—they were aberrations. Since his writing seems so effortless it was strange to learn from the play that Ransome had a hard time getting started as a storyteller. Indeed, of *Swallows and Amazons*, he said: 'I could not help writing it. It almost wrote itself'. It reads that way.

As a child, growing up in a Magic Kingdom (although she did not then know it was one), Glynis tended to look sideways at Arthur Ransome and his books, and at other books of the same genre, as part of a complacent, middle-class, world of privately educated children with whom she felt nothing in common. But then, regardless of how she felt about all that, the fact was that she lived in a Magic Kingdom and had no need of others.

There was a time when, before going away from here—back to London, back to Durham, back to Washington, back to Bogota—I would scurry around saying goodbye to each special place. But that was when the known boundaries of the Kingdom were dictated by how far I walked or, a bit later, how far I bicycled. Over the years, although those boundaries have shifted a bit, the fact of having—as I like to think—explored every road, footpath, and track within it has gradually made it impossible to go around saying goodbye. It would take days. It would be pointless. Besides, I have learned to trust the special places; they won't go away while I'm gone. It's enough to know they are all there.

Despite my implied claim to know the details of the Magic Kingdom at least as well as the back of my hand and probably better because, if other people are like me, they don't spend a lot of time looking at the backs of their hands—which are things that one sees but does not study—the truth is that I continue to discover new things.

Just the other day, passing a house at the end of Northfield Lane in Wells, which I must have passed thousands of times before, I realized it was made of red carrstone, an alien material in these parts. It was of course made of carrstone the first time I saw it thirty years ago. It has been made of carrstone ever since it was built in, I would guess, about1910.

In the same way, the old centre of Cley was exactly where it is now long before I knew Norfolk existed. Somehow, though, I had never thought about the relationship between the church, which is close to what was the village centre, and the present centre of activity along the coast road. It was years before I explored the oldest part of Cley; no longer Next-the-Marsh, let alone Next-the-Sea.

So some things are new because you don't see them but were there all the time. Others are new because things change physically, and I am, I think, more alert to such changes. This year for example ... the old whelkhouses at the far end of East End in Wells—where, for much longer than I can remember, the Cox family boiled their whelks every day before shipping them off by rail (and after the railway was closed, by road) to their markets in London and Paris—have been pulled down. Some of the other whelkhouses are still functioning but the distinctive smell of East End—a combination of a Monday morning wash-house and fish braised in herbs—is not what it used to be... There is a new barn conversion near the Manor House in Binham, work on which was just starting when we were last here ..., an adjacent site to that conversion, facing Howells' Superstores, has been cleared for building (What will be there next year?)... the village shop in Langham has a splendid new name, Wizards End Stores, and now sells astrological advice as well as soap, frozen dinners, and postage stamps ...; a parking fee has been introduced on the quay at Morston, to help pay for the costs of National Trust maintenance ...; new signs have been put up all over the place announcing the presence of English Nature that weren't here two years ago...; there are hand-carved and unpainted wooden signs to footpaths that make me feel better about taking straight lines across barley fields where the right of way shown on the Ordnance Survey map is invisible because it is ploughed up every year...; there is a vast increase in the number of rabbits and a smaller increase in the number of hares since last time we were here ...; and there is the never-ending reconfiguration of Scolt Head Island, Holkham Gap, Wells Beach, and Blakeney Point.

The discovery of each of these changes, subtle or brazen, good (in my eyes) or bad, permanent or temporary, obvious or concealed, brings a thrill of pleasure or a *frisson* of anxiety. Change is, after all, a constant. The Magic Kingdom is not caught in a time-warp. Like the rest of the world, it moves on. Enough is unchanged to reassure me it is unchanging. Enough is new to tell me it is alive.

The creeks that bring mystery to the saltmarsh are where they have been as long as I have known them. The sand and mud on the harbour bottom and in Wells channel have shifted so much I must learn them again—for the first time—every year. The hedges that protect the fields, shelter nesting birds, and nourish hovering butterflies are in the same places they were in when I made maps of field boundaries as an undergraduate. The parish churches, seemingly as old as time itself, continue to watch over the now pagan communities they once regulated. The ruined cloister of the old priory is empty, but I remember the massive oak tree that grew there (until it came down in a great storm three years ago) because, on the wall before me, there is a photograph of us sitting under it with our then two-child family that Campbell MacCallum took in the mid-1970s.

The shops in Fakenham from which we have been buying things for years are still there: the Wooden Horse, Fakenham Hardware, Boots, Woolworths, Powells Sports, and Peatlings. But Peatlings has changed almost beyond recognition since last time; you can now go down to the cellar and browse there as long as you want among the claret and port.

The fish-and-chip shop in Holt has also been remodelled but the same people are still running it. And most of the 'For Sale' signs that were dotted around the countryside two years ago are still there, recording the collapse of the property market.

So the balance of change and continuity seems—to me anyway—about right. We can go to the same places we have always gone to. We can drink beer in the same pubs and eat in the same restaurants. We can sail in the same boats. And walk on the same paths. And thus far, because nobody has died or gone away, see the same friends. Yet there is always something, however little, that is new and different. We are of course very fortunate that the whole of the Magic Kingdom is actively looked after by the combined forces of the National Trust, the Nature Conservancy, English Heritage, English Nature, the Norfolk Naturalists Trust and the Norfolk County Council. And that their efforts are supported by thousands of volunteers who also love this place. Most of them I do not know. They are the people I see, binoculars in hand, looking for birds at Cley; the people I greet on footpaths; the people who belong to organizations like the Burnham Harbour Trust. And, of course, they do not know me. But I am immensely grateful to them because, I understand, while I am somewhere else, they will if need be defend every building worth keeping and protect every foot of the marshes and the foreshore.

11 August

I have just looked over what I have written so far. It's grown quite fast, but I'm afraid I have not said all I want to say I'm nearly out of time. Fantasy: I write not one, but several books about North Norfolk. Reality: last night, the Federal Express man brought me a package from Washington and within hours my colleague was on the phone asking for comments on the paper that came in the package. Just as well I am still fascinated by the topic. Later today I shall read it and then call back with my reactions.

But, comparatively at least, this is a trifling matter. In other years, it seems that hardly a day has passed that I have not heard from the Bank. Before we got a telephone installed at Binham, I would get a message through my mother-in-law in Wells to call the Bank. Then, I would collect enough coins to get connected and have surreal conversations from a phone box on the edge of a cornfield about abstruse issues that seemed quite unrelated to where I was. The telephone is like that, I suppose—at least over a long distance—because the people who are talking to each other are necessarily ignorant of the other's exact reality: 'What's the weather like where you are?' Calling across town, or even across country (except humongous countries like Russia and the USA), you are in the same time zone, the same weather system, and have read the same papers while eating similar things for breakfast that morning.

The worst moment was our twenty-fifth wedding anniversary, when Glynis and I drove to Dolgellau, where we spent part of our honeymoon. We had just reached the hotel when there was a call from Washington. Glynis went for a walk.

If You Build It They Might Come (but then again they might not)

North Norfolk is more fashionable than it used to be. A lot more if you go back thirty years. Noticeably more if you go back only five years. The completion of the M 25 and the M 11, and the 'dualling' (an intransitive verb, meaning the act of turning a two-lane road into a four-lane highway, that is as yet in neither the Oxford nor Webster's dictionary) of other roads have made it easier to get here. But that really only applies to those who come and go, the weekenders.

A separate set of issues arises from the fact that people are living longer and staying healthier into their seventies. There are more and more of them. 'Retirees', they are called in the States. But how much do they really contribute to the pressure on the environment? Just by being here? And whether they do or not, what else do they contribute? Are they active or passive forces of change? What, in fact, are the implications of the *greying* of the Magic Kingdom?

Some of those who retire here find that places that were golden in summer are dreary in the long winter. Since we arrived a month ago, we have looked at no fewer than three houses that are on the market because their owners are moving to France, where winters are warmer than they are in Norfolk. And I don't think one could blame Mr Mayle for that because only one of them is going to Provence.

But most of the retirees seem to adjust to the rhythm of living in the country, year round. So they stay. Few of them have large disposable incomes. Typically, once they've sold their houses in Leicester, London or Liverpool, they have savings of perhaps twenty or thirty thousand pounds. Not a large fortune these days. So it is not primarily the retirees who bid up prices and expect to find a decent selection of champagne in Howells' Superstores.

Their cultural perspectives are, by and large, as modest as their means. Fifteen years or so ago—in the late 1970s—Michael Gough and others who lived in North Norfolk at weekends conceived of and launched the Wells Centre. Its purpose was to offer a year-round programme of drama, music, film, lectures, and exhibitions. It struggled on for nearly ten years before it collapsed. The lesson is obvious: absent a solid base of demand in the market area, and initiatives such as this are a waste of time, money, and hopes.

In retrospect, it seems obvious that there was no reason to expect that simply because the Wells Centre was built, people would come to it. They didn't. There was, at first, a lot of curiosity. But once that faded, support dwindled and interest dried up. The now famous phrase: 'If you build it they will come', was coined for a baseball stadium in an Iowa cornfield. And with baseball you can perhaps assume that if they *do* come, they will keep on coming. Not so for the Wells Centre. They (the local population including the retirees) came a few times out of a sense of curiosity and a typically English sense of duty. Then they stopped coming and stayed at home with the television instead.

Now I have to confess that, in a way, I am glad it failed. Not because I am anti-art. But because the whole thing was a foreign invention. The prime movers lived elsewhere most of the time. They had thin local connexions, mostly with people like themselves. And the enterprise was, more than anything, a monument to what *they* thought the local people should want, on the grounds that if they were them (the local people) that is what they would want for themselves. That sort of thinking rarely pans out. It is arrogant. It is unrealistic. And it is a poor basis for business decisions of any kind.

There were no doubt some who thought, if art can succeed in north-east Suffolk, why not in North Norfolk? After all, did Benjamin Britten and Peter Pears bother with market research before they launched the Aldeburgh Festival in what must have been a pretty rocky economic environment? Of course not. They just did it. And they were right to do it. But perhaps they knew the local population better than Michael Gough and his friends knew theirs. And perhaps it was in fact different because there may indeed be reason to think that north-east Suffolk, which is much nearer London than North Norfolk, had a bigger sprinkling of actual or potential arts patrons.

When Glynis and I had our first boat, the red canoe *Shalom*, one of our favourite things was to launch it in to Wells harbour on a fine summer evening. We'd paddle up the creek or down the channel until we could see the whole town spread along the waterfront as the sun set over Holkham to our right. It was then, and still is, a lovely moment; one to savour in the mind like an Islay malt on the palate. And we talked (perhaps it was only once or twice but I am tempted to say, 'We used to talk', as though we did it all the time—but then, 'used to' is a notoriously treacherous phrase) about what would happen to Wells. Would it become a mini-Yarmouth? Or would the RSPB and the other middle-class organizations with conservationist values and four-letter acronyms prevail?

Thirty years later, the answer is clear. Neither. The mode continues to be co-existence. Wells remains an eclectic mixture of honkytonk and conservatism (note the small 'c'). It continues to appeal to those who obviously want *some* of what is offered by the cluster of bingo parlours, video arcades, and fast-food places on the quay, but who presumably only want a *bit* of that or they would go somewhere like Yarmouth or Hunstanton, where they could have a lot of it. Presumably therefore they want something else besides: the sort of something else the conservatives themselves want, although neither faction seems to see it that way, preferring instead to keep their heads firmly implanted in buckets of class prejudice.

Pretty much everywhere else in the Magic Kingdom, the conservatives have confirmed their victories. Not that the outcome was ever in doubt. I dare say many of them would like the gaudy bits of Wells quay to disappear and then there would be no blemishes at all. The Magic Kingdom could be consecrated entirely for the enjoyment of those they may think of as 'the right kind of people'.

I have never been inside one of Don Gray's amusement places on Wells quay, and I feel neither an urge nor a need to do so. But I am glad it is the way it is because it is real. It is alive. And the second great threat we face, besides pressure on resources, is that the villages of the Magic Kingdom that are still alive will die. Not from excessive pressure. Not from over-population. But because a large part of that population is elderly, infirm, and either disinclined to go outside or incapable of going outside, especially in winter.

You do not have to look far beyond the surface of things to understand there are already several dead communities in the Magic Kingdom and that others are in danger of dying. Take Hindringham, a large village (of about six hundred people) with no pub and no shops, yet many new and, for the most part, mediocre houses and bungalows; is it a living community or a dormitory for Fakenham? Or take either of the (Great or Little) Snorings: are they dead or are they only pretending to be dead? And what about Field Dalling? Is the sense of emptiness I get there the product of a too-superficial impression, or is there a deathly smell in the air, Saxlingham and Field Dalling Village Hall notwithstanding? These villages, and others like them—the larger ones more than the smaller ones, I think—are, to all intents and purposes, places where people sleep but not where people work; where old people die but where no children are born; from which young people leave but to which few return.

The realist in me says there is no earthly—or for that matter heavenly—use in railing against demography. But the consequences of the Magic Kingdom becoming a cross between a retirement community and a weekend-cum-summer playground for second-home owners are frightening. The economics of agriculture and the fact that in other branches of economic activity—except for the so-called 'Holiday Industry'—North Norfolk is mainly remarkable for its comparative disadvantages mean there are few sources of work now. And there may be even fewer in the offing.

The process of making this area *unreal* is itself very real and it cannot easily be halted The pragmatist in me says, since you can't stop them, join them. Turn a weakness into a strength. Let the natural momentum of demographic trends and economic realities lead to sound policy choices.

In the early 1960s, when Dr Beeching—as he was then known—swung his axe and lopped off the North Norfolk line that ran from Norwich, via Dereham and Fakenham with stops at such gems of places as North Elmham and County School, there were howls of protest, that I would now describe as futile and useless. It seemed different then. 'What about the people without cars?' we said; there would be regular buses, *they* said. 'What about attracting light industry to Wells?', we said; if it wants to come it will come and if it doesn't, it won't (actually, on a very small scale, it did) *they* said.

The succession of uses to which North Norfolk has historically been put reflects changes in both technologies and values. The demographic trend towards an ageing and less active population reflects social change and medical progress. These realities will pose a unique challenge to those who must shape the framework of laws, bylaws, and incentives that will govern the market for the economic resources of the Magic Kingdom in the 1990s and beyond.

In a fundamental sense, there is nothing really new in the tension between ancient and modern; conservation and development; and conflicting ideas about what the beaches, the fields, the marshes, and the woodlands should be used for and who should use them. In the eighteenth century the battle was over enclosures. In the nineteenth century it was over the mechanization of agriculture. In the twentieth century it has been over economic and social changes punctuated by two wars. In the twenty-first century it will be partly about managing pressure on resources.

But there is something else: finding ways and means to ensure the communities of the Magic Kingdom stay alive—week in, week out, and year after year—and do not live only at weekends and in the short months of summer. Double jeopardy, as one of my colleagues would say; the choice between the proverbial rock and the really (Americans like to say 'real' in this context), hard place.

I sense that the 'greying' of North Norfolk is a counterpoint to its greening and that it is both a threat and an illusion. The threat is that a growing part of the population will have lived most of its life elsewhere, and will make demands on the local economy that it may be hard pressed to meet. In return, current evidence suggests that by reason of frailty and indifference, this population will not contribute much to the community. I know full well there are exceptions. I know too that because 'foreigners' are not always made welcome, it is quite unfair to blame them.

But the 'grey' population, much of it now snuggled together in enclave communities of small new houses built primarily with them in mind, is also an illusion. It is there but not there. Its members are enumerated in the census and the electoral roll but do not, because they are indifferent, infirm, or feel unwanted, participate in the life of the community. The towns and villages therefore have less and less life and gradually wither away. The process has started. The question now: is it inexorable?

15 August

We leave tomorrow for London. And for once, our retreat should be more or less orderly. Usually, we have gone straight from here to Heathrow, then direct to Washington. This time, we are staying a couple of nights with Richard and Liz in Lambeth. And on Sunday afternoon, Cameron and I are going to see the America Bowl at Wembley. On Monday, we'll show Cameron and Catriona something of London before we fly back on Tuesday. I'll deliver the Volvo to the shipping agents on the way to the airport and, all being well, it'll be in Washington within the month.

One year, the day we were leaving, I decided to make a quick trip to the Dump to get rid of some bits and pieces that had accumulated in our carport. I had been saying for four weeks: 'I must take those things to the Dump' and here I was, on our last morning, getting up early to do something I should have done before. There were some long iron bars I had to get rid of, so I left the tailgate up and open. Our local Dump is on the Wells–Walsingham road. No traffic on the way there; still too early. I overshot the entrance. And then backed up to it, forgetting about the tailgate and not seeing the iron bar across the entrance, six feet off the ground. Glass and metal rained on the roof. I couldn't believe what I'd done. An hour later at the Volvo dealership in Fakenham: 'How are you?', I said with what I fancy was a sick grin. 'Better than your Volvo', he said. We got it back three months later, good as new. But I still cringe whenever I pass the Dump.

I still have no idea about whether this will find a publisher. I think it's the kind of book I'd like to read myself. But how many other people share my taste? Since I started on it after I arrived in July, it's more or less shaped itself. Things have just come to mind whenever I have sat down to write. There was no outline. No plan. Only an urge that suddenly, this year, became urgent. Even though I haven't known in advance what I would write about I do know that I want to end on what I'd have to call a serious note.

Writing this journal over a month of reflecting on as many summers as there are days in a month that I have spent here, has made me think—for almost the first time, and certainly for the first time in a long time —about the future of the Magic Kingdom. For thirty years, I have, as the saying goes, been 'present to the moment' whenever I've been here. Although there was a time when I tried to plan our holidays, the context was the next few weeks. Now, I'm wondering about the next few years and the years beyond them. How will the Magic Kingdom be when I am ready to retire and spend much more time here? Will my grandchildren—assuming my own *children produce some, biologically and actuarily a reasonable assumption—know it as their parents—my children—have known it? I am certain they will be encouraged to, because both Carey and Caitlin have declared their allegiance and Catriona and Cameron are in the process of becoming attached.*

The last time I thought much about the future of the Magic Kingdom, I was a student at University College. At that stage, I didn't realize it was, in fact, a Magic Kingdom. I was already enthralled but it took me a long time to understand why. And the things I wrote about then did not include issues arising from the pressure of people on a fragile environment. Nor issues arising from a greying population.

I'm sure there are others who have given a lot of thought to these topics and realize that the character of North Norfolk is being transformed. But I have the feeling that a lot of the people who live here all the time do not, precisely because they live here all the time and thus lack perspective. It seems to me that, in historical terms, the Magic Kingdom is probably changing faster now than at any time since the eighteenth-century enclosure movement transfigured its economic geography in a few decades. It is certainly not the place it was when I first came here thirty years ago.

Indeed, it will never be the same again. The old men in cloth caps and collarless shirts have gone for ever. So have the old women who wore hats and aprons to go shopping. And the characters like Barty Edwards who walked twice a day, winter and summer, from Warham to Wells and back again, wearing a battered top hat and a bright red neckerchief

It's not that I want them back. But I need to remember them because they tell the story of time. And unless one looks back, one cannot look forward. It is pointless thinking about the future if there are no points of reference. Thirty years ago, North Norfolk—'on the way to nowhere', as they say here—was a bit of a place apart. It was not difficult to get to. In fact, if you were without a car it was easier to get here then than it is now; there was a train. Yet it was certainly more remote in other ways. Separate and distinctive, it marched defiantly and quietly to the subtle beat of a different drummer from the rest of the country and, in some respects, the rest of the county.

North Norfolk is now a place where churches are buildings you visit to hear piano recitals and string quartets; where Brie and champagne and caviare have come to stay on grocers' shelves; and where an increasing proportion of adult men do not tuck their shirts in their underpants.

But the biggest change is the evolution of new relationships between the sons (and of course the daughters) and the lovers. Between the North Norfolk people, and the people of North Norfolk. Between the Old Guard and the New Wave. Between those for whom the unwritten rules about what it takes to be classified as a 'local' person carry great weight, and those who do not even know such rules (and the discrimination that goes with them) exist.

Those who were born here and, give or take a few years, have always lived here make this place what it is. Indeed, if they *were not here,* it *would not be here. On one level, it is perfectly true that the magic of the Magic Kingdom comes from the marshes, the beaches, the woods, the birds, the flowers, and the animals. And from the fields, the hedgerows, the lanes, the houses, the churches, the shops, and the pubs. But it also comes from the people who live here all the time, and who guarantee continuity, take care of maintenance, and enforce protection. Without them, it would not be the same. Not at all.*

Thirty, even twenty, years ago, they were ascendent, dominant, and in their element. They knew who they were. They made the rules. They set the trends. They ran the businesses. And the local government.

Not any more. For one thing, the truly local people are now outnumbered. In some villages (and here I do not of course include myself, because I only married into the community), there are fewer sons (and daughters) than lovers. Some of the latter group belong to the North Norfolk clan of the great tribe of weekenders who decamp from the cities of the south and the Midlands on Friday evening and go back to them on Sunday night or Monday morning.

Other lovers (qualifications: an uncontrolled urge to imitate the inimitable accent of Norfolk, including a compulsive need to say 'bootyful' for beautiful, 'bor' for boy, and 'yew' for you) do not come and go. They only come. Because when they go, they are dead. Not surprising because they come here to die. Accordingly, if North Norfolk were in America this would be a great place to go into the business of funeral homes and private cemeteries and crematoria. But all the cemeteries here are public. That prompts the rather radical question (for some people): why not bury people where they spend most of their lives? If that were done retroactively in North Norfolk, there would be capacity enough for people entitled to local burial well in to the next century, without digging another grave.

What is at issue is decidedly—as they say in the computer business—non-trivial. (Translation: 'it is important'; you may have noticed that people in the computer business tend to make everything they say more mysterious than it really is, and 'non-trivial' certainly sounds *as though it might mean something out of the ordinary). What is at stake is nothing less than the future existence of the Magic Kingdom. Not because it might be consumed by the millenial flood. Nor because it might be overrun by people. But because there may be too few authentically local people (a.k.a. North Norfolk People) to keep it going. The threat is like having Hamlet without the Prince of Denmark; gin without juniper; gardening without dirty hands; bricks without straw. The prospect is North Norfolk without (real) North Norfolk people, part of a seamless web of places that were once rural but are now living museums, that depict rural life as it never was.*

So I shall end not with a call to arms, because that would be silly, but with a warning: it could happen here! *Oh yes. And since I can't resist the temptation, with a few well-intentioned suggestions of what might be done about it.*

In the End

For lunch today at the Crown in Wells, I had whitebait. For some reason I only seem to come across whitebait in England. It added one more treat to the list of foods and drinks I have enjoyed in the last month. Since I don't recall ever having heard of, let alone eaten, whitebait as a child, I must have had it for the first time when I was in my twenties. Somewhere in England.

It cannot be coincidental that so many grown men and women I know get a kick from the food and drink of childhood and young adulthood. I wonder: is that a peculiarly English phenomenon, or a universal one? It's odd that I have spent all but two years of my working life in multi-cultural and international environments, yet have no idea whether that's so.

From time to time, sitting in a meeting of, say, ten people at the Bank in Washington, I'm struck by the fact they may have ten different nationalities and come from three different continents. Nobody ever comments on that because we all take it for granted. But I suppose I could ask a few people casually about the food and drink of their childhoods. If I do, my guess is I'll find it's a universal pattern, though it may be accentuated among the English because of their youthful exposure to institutional food. I have found that the food concerned is remarkably classless in this class-heavy society; for some reason, we all seem to have grown up on baked beans, sausages, treacle pudding and spotted dick (known in some places as spotted dog).

After lunch, walking across the Buttlands, there were some people playing what they might have called baseball. It would not have passed muster in the States where that game is known, almost reverently, as 'America's Pastime'. Rounders would be more like it. There were some other people eating a late lunch on a bench. The Buttlands are so called because it was there, in the Middle Ages, that the men of Wells practised archery, the butts being the targets, in what was then the most advanced art of war. Binham also has a buttlands. That suggests, although I have not followed up on the idea, that each village set aside an area where the local population could keep their hand (should it be 'hands' or 'eyes *and* hands') in shape to defend home and hearth—or whatever else they had to defend—against the predations of thugs, invaders, and warlords. The latter included bishops, abbots, and other holy men who found religion and aggression compatible; and, likely enough, some of the crusaders who helped Richard knock sense into the Turks in the thirteenth century refined their skills on the buttlands of North Norfolk.

Anyway, back to the people having lunch and playing rounders.

Glynis said she felt sorry for them because there wasn't much for them to do on a blustery and rather chilly day like today with temperatures in the sixties when they couldn't go to the beach, unless they wanted to wear more clothes than anybody should ever wear on a beach. I said I didn't feel sorry for them at all. If they wanted to spend all day, every day, on the beach, they should go somewhere else.

Glynis said that was like Marie Antoinette saying people should eat cake if they didn't have bread. That's the first time (as far as I know) I've been compared to Marie Antoinette (or, more precisely, something I've said has been compared to something she is rumoured to have said at a time of crisis). So I defended myself by saying I didn't mean that they should go instead to the Maldives or the Virgin Islands or even Benidorm because I realized one reason they came here was that it was cheaper than Brighton and quieter than Yarmouth.

My point was that it is futile to complain. (And how, by the way, did she know they were complaining? They might like being on the Buttlands.) People who come to the Magic Kingdom can't expect it to provide the kind of weather that guarantees a suntan within seven days or for that matter seven weeks. This is, after all, a damp island in the high northern latitudes and rain and cold are always on the cards.

I went on to point out that there are dozens, no hundreds, of things to do in the Magic Kingdom besides sitting on the beach or sitting on the Buttlands. They could do something different every day for a month, or even a year, if they used their eyes to read maps and their imaginations to create new adventures. A reasonable response, I thought, even though I knew there was something wrong with it on which I couldn't quite put my finger.

Later, thinking over what Glynis had said to me and I had said to her, I put my finger on the problem. It was all very well for me to talk about alternatives, but I was drawing on three decades of knowledge. Part of what I cherish about North Norfolk is a sense of belonging, of knowing my way around, of having a key to the Magic Kingdom. I am very fortunate. So are my children, who, although some of them were born an ocean away from it, have inherited a birthright of sorts from their mother. This sense of belonging and the knowledge that goes with it is, for me, a fundamental part of the magic. The question to which my finger pointed was whether it was also an *essential* part of the magic. Is the Magic Kingdom magical for those who have not found the way to its secret soul? Is it possible to grasp the magic of North Norfolk without being, in a more than transitory way, part of its human fabric? Can visitors like those on the Buttlands discover all it has to offer?

In the lapse of a day, a week, or even a month, they cannot. But North Norfolk is sufficiently open and transparent for even a casual visitor to appreciate it, if not in full, then in part. Clearly, some Magic Kingdoms are more open than others. A few years ago, we decided to show our children something of Scotland and the Lake District instead of staying put in Norfolk. We rented a draughty baronial mansion in Caithness and a farmhouse in Kentdale, each for a week. It was not one of our better vacations. It rained most of the time in both places. The houses were certainly big enough (the one in Caithness was actually enormous), but rather run down. But the real frustration, for me at least, was that I did not have and could not find, the keys to either kingdom. I had, of course, being me, loaded up on guidebooks and maps. But many of our expeditions—the exceptions being those to places in the Lakes I had been to when I was at school—turned out to be less than magical mystery tours. The idea of discovering new places every day was tantalizing. But a lot of the choices we made seemed to be mediocre, and often we wished we had done something else. It became painfully obvious that our problem was not a shortage of information; it was a shortage of knowledge grounded in experience. And the fact is, allowing that some places are more transparent than others, you do not acquire that kind of knowledge in a week or a month.

As Prospero showed, islands—if they are bountiful as well as bounded—can make enchanting kingdoms. By the end of the very first July we spent on Martha's Vineyard, we felt we had already begun to love it. We sensed we were starting out on a lasting relationship, superficial, recently acquired, and half-digested though our knowledge of it was. The Magic Kingdom of the Vineyard, compared with some others (North Norfolk included), simply lay there in the warm summer waters off Cape Cod, waiting to entrap its visitor in an awesome spell that, once cast, seemed never to weaken. Scale obviously had something to do with it because the magic of the Vineyard derived, in part, from the fact that it was large enough to boast variety but small enough to be intimate.

The importance of scale in shaping our capacity to grasp the magic of the Magic Kingdoms was driven home to me when I thought about my experiences in an entirely different sort of place: an art gallery or a museum. There you are, in the Prado or the Hermitage for the first (and who knows, perhaps the only) time. You have a choice. Rush around in two or three hours and when you leave, slap a 'Been There, Done That' sticker in your figurative travel log. Or decide, preferably in advance, what you most want to see, and spend all your time in one room. None of the paintings in whatever room that turns out to be was conceived or executed in five minutes or less. And if they are worth viewing at all, it will take even an untutored brain like mine at least twenty or thirty minutes to begin to understand each one of them. It's odd, isn't it, that we expect to spend an hour and a half understanding a film, three hours understanding a play, and perhaps several days understanding a book, yet expect to see all there is to see in an oil painting or a water-colour in a matter of minutes or even seconds?

However, it is not only a matter of scale. The more complex, subtle, and opaque the joys and wonders of a place—whether we are talking about the Louvre or North Norfolk—the more time and effort you must make to penetrate its secrets and be touched by its magic. Among the Magic Kingdoms that I have—in varying degrees—known, the Magic Kingdom of North Norfolk is neither the least nor the most reluctant to bare its soul. It does not overwhelm you. Its beauties are not those of a striking, statuesque, long-tressed maiden. It is not Switzerland. Or the Grand Tetons National Park in Wyoming. Or Macchu Pichu. It doesn't knock you off your feet or even your bicycle. I have seen places that have, quite literally, taken my breath away, and when I got it back all I could say was, 'Wow' or something similar. I doubt the heart of anybody seeing North Norfolk for the first time has skipped a beat. A casual visitor may find it charming because it is not 'spoiled', or boring because there is nothing in the least dramatic about it.

Yet I believe that anybody coming here in search of magic will find some. Not all of it the first time. Or the second. Or the thirtieth. Because it goes on revealing itself for ever. But everyone who seeks for it will find some of it. Even the most fleeting visitor, given time to spend and maps to read—all the information you really need is on them—can find at least some of the places and the people that make the Magic Kingdom magical.

Just last night, over dinner, Miranda Crafer was telling me about a man who regularly brings his caravan to the Manor Farm paddock. He had described to her what he had done and where he had been in ten days, and how he hated the idea of going back to Leicester at the end of the week. It was quite obvious he had found his way around, had unlocked the gates, and had indeed found some magic. You could, said Miranda, see it in his eyes.

So I think I was right about the people on the Buttlands today who seemed to have nothing to do and nowhere to go. They were not nowhere. They were where we were. And they had something to do. They were playing rounders and eating lunch. It may still be true that they would have preferred to be on the beach. But they were not huddled in their caravans on the beach camp site, muttering about the weather.

The man in Miranda's paddock also proves that the desire and capacity to love places is a function of neither education nor income. Glynis's grandfather, who at the age of eighty returned to his dingle on the Welsh border to die, left school at twelve and spent most of his life mending railway tracks. He was neither educated in any formal sense, nor wealthy in any conventional sense. But he was wise in the ways of the countrysides of both his Magic Kingdom and this Magic Kingdom. And his knowledge represented another kind of wealth that made him a rich man. The capacity to love, cherish, and understand places has little or nothing to do with bank balances or academic credentials.

If the passing wanderer can expect to get *something* out of simply being here, what does it take to get as much as there is to be taken from the Magic Kingdom?

Quite clearly, just *living* here is *not* enough. To become part of the fabric of this rural society—and not just an appreciative observer of its landscapes and manscapes—means more than having a permanent address in North Norfolk. It even means more than living at that address all the time. What then does it mean? What does it take to become part of the woof to the warp of the history of the Magic Kingdom? A rhetorical question to which the same answer, or a very similar one, would hold true for any Magic Kingdom.

There is quite a range of pretenders to the status of soulmate and lover of Magic Kingdoms. At one end of the scale is the casual visitor who, by and large, cannot expect to capture more than the scent of a magical trail in the lapse of a few days or even a few weeks. At the other end of the scale there is the the native: born here, lives here, plans to die here—a part and parcel of the place.

Between them are three categories of people with some claim to be keepers of the keys. First, there is the immigrant who comes to live here full-time, having previously lived somewhere else. The retiree belongs to this group, as does the relocated worker and his family. The second group consists of occasional residents, who may come here only in summer for a few weeks; the 'Summer People' who swell the population of the Vineyard from nine thousand to fifty thousand are a good example. The third group consists of the periodic residents. They include the 'Weekenders' who throughout the year, but usually much less in winter than in summer, arrive on Friday and leave on Sunday. It also includes the 'Weekly Commuters' whose families live here all the time, but who come only at weekends, staying in a *pied-à-terre* during the week. And it includes the dreaded species of 'Daily Commuter' who voluntarily dies twice a day while his or her body is shipped to London and back. Only one of them (the Daily Commuter) is not yet found in North Norfolk.

The other day, at 'lunchtime'—which is a euphemism for the

hours between twelve and two when many of our friends are simultaneously overcome by an urgent yet predictable need to take urgent measures against dehydration in the Crown—there was a lively discussion about whether Wells Sailing Club, despite its simplicity and down-to-earthness, was at the same time, and without meaning to be, exclusive and unfriendly. Does it put strangers off? Are there implicit rules about who belongs and who half-belongs? One viewpoint was that it does and that there are. The other viewpoint was horrified defence. I said I did not find the sailing club at all closed. To the contrary. But thinking further, I can also see the other point of view. I, after all, had an acquired advantage in that my wife and her family are as authentically local as you can be. It was not surprising I had never encountered barriers. Suppose, instead, I had walked in off the street? Would I have been embraced, welcomed, and encouraged as I felt I was? I'm not sure.

This question is important in a much larger context than that of the sailing club because, as a practical matter, it has a lot to do with whether people who come here from elsewhere feel comfortable and fit in. In the past, people who moved on retirement to the Magic Kingdom found local organizations were pretty much in local hands. They were run by people with impeccable credentials, who welcomed strangers, but on their terms. The sensible stranger understood the subtexts and the subliminal messages, bided his time, spoke when spoken to, and adjusted to local traditions and customs. The stupid stranger immediately saw ways to make things more effective and efficient and, sometimes, with the best of good intentions, said so. Generally speaking, not a wise move.

There's nothing unique or surprising about that. Throughout the world, local custom tends to prevail. In much of it, indeed, natives are hostile to strangers. Sometimes because they threaten. Sometimes because they are different. But usually for no other reason than that they came from somewhere else, the accepted word for which around here is simply 'away".

'*They* say', said the woman with an East Midlands accent, who had come to live in Wells when her husband had retired nearly ten years earlier, 'that you can't park there.' Ignoring her, the local woman said loudly to her passenger, 'Just who does she think she is; she's only been here five minutes.' Although she was right (there *was* a 'No Parking' sign outside the health centre) she was also wrong (because the parking lot was empty and the health centre was about to close and common sense said it was perfectly reasonable to park there). But that wasn't the point. She was being uppity. She was behaving as people from 'away' are not supposed to behave. She did not know her place.

The problem with suburbs the world over is that they are, for the most part, new. They did not exist a hundred or even fifty years ago. They are architectural conveniences. You can live in them for years without knowing your neighbours or having anything to do with them. Rural villages are supposed to be different. And in many ways, they are. It is conceptually impossible to live in a village that is not a community. In a population, like Binham's, of only three hundred or so, it is as yet inconceivable that somebody who noticed they had not seen one of their neighbours that day would not check to see all was well. It is impossible to imagine that somebody could die—as happens all too often in cities—without anybody knowing, or caring. The Greek idea of *comunitas* is after all, about caring, interdependency, mutuality, and support. How could you have a community of three hundred people without *comunitas*?

Well, it's possible. Indeed, it is happening in North Norfolk as the local population continues to decline, as young people continue to move away, as more and more village schools close and are consolidated a bus ride away, and as social customs become more centred around the immediate family and have less to do with neighbours.

The 'dead' villages are likely to stay dead although miracles do happen as new shops open and closed pubs start serving beer again. In Stiffkey, for example, both the Red Lion and the Post Office shop have recently come back to life. And the Three Horseshoes in Warham, which might as well have been dead for the last thirty years, has been transformed since 1990. There is something infinitely depressing about driving through Hindringham or Little Snoring at night and finding them, almost literally, empty. Not only because neither of them has a pub. But because so many of the cottages and houses are dark.

They are not dark because electricity has not yet been connected or because the people who live there have gone to bed early. They are dark because their owners are in London, or Nottingham, or Sheffield. In our own micro-community in Binham, there are sixteen houses. Only three of them are permanently occupied, all by retirees. Now, in August most of them will be inhabited at weekends and more than half will be populated all week round. But by November, thirteen will be dark every evening. A few people will come down at Christmas. And then they will be empty and dark again until the spring.

Fifty years ago, smoke would have risen from every chimney in the village every evening of the year. There would have been lights of some sort—not then electric—in every window. Now, there are more houses but fewer lights, more property owners but fewer residents. And Binham is comparatively well off. It has a

Post Office, a 'superstores' that sells everything including gasoline, a butcher's shop, and a sixteenth-century pub. Despite the lopsidedness of our part of the village, its resident population is also proportionately larger than in most villages. It even has an active (and locally run) parish council.

What killed the countryside of southern England after the Second World War was the strange and even willing acceptance of commuting over ridiculous distances between home and work. If people were not willing to die on schedule twice a day, five days a week, Sussex and Hampshire and Dorset would not have been converted into up-scale bedrooms. There are now people who travel daily between London and Norwich. The roads—and the public resources available to improve them—being what they are, I see little risk, at least in the foreseeable future, that people will commute regularly between London and the Magic Kingdom. Death will not come from that direction.

It is the retirees that worry me. There is a real risk that what I perceive as a stand-off between local people on the one hand and the retirees on the other will continue. And either the newcomers will turn over and go back to sleep and have nothing of substance to do with the community. Or they will be active within their own enclaves of retirees. Or they will take over. There is evidence of all three responses.

The first and second outcomes mean the communities will continue to die, and fifty years from now you will not be able to tell the difference between a North Norfolk village and a suburban housing estate built yesterday to accommodate people coming to it from hither and yon. Thirty years ago, when I first came here, the difference was so palpable, it was like stepping from the air conditioned cabin of a jetliner into a blast of thick, hot tropical air at one of the relatively few airports without ramps that let you walk straight in to the terminal.

Some of the sense of *comunitas* is left, but there is less by the year; something that we, as regular visitors but non-residents, may notice more than others. And once it has evaporated, there will be no more. Communities are bound by trust and confidence and experience. They grow slowly and organically.

I see only one real option for the future. The newcomers who were not born here, did not raise families here, and do not work here or anywhere else, must be let in. Communities that, historically, have survived for hundreds of years, have survived because they have understood and accepted that the future is not the past. There are some constants. There is some continuity. There are traditions. There is the old. And the familiar. But there is novelty. Innovation. Invention. Experimentation. Change.

The challenge facing the communities of the Magic Kingdom in the 1990s and into the next century will be to embrace the reality that its comparative economic advantage will lie in being a place where people will live the third age of their lives and must become integrated. That means they must be accepted as leaders if they offer leadership, enjoined as followers if they offer followership, and be made to feel welcome and wanted. The English are not, in my opinion, very good at that. Americans, all of whom are transplantees anyway, do it much more sincerely. The easy-going style and enthusiastic greeting, 'How do you spell your name?' (said in a way that suggests the asker really wants to know) that Europeans associate with Americans, is a natural product of a society founded on the premise of horizontal mobility. But the inhabitants of the Magic Kingdom must, I think, recognize a change in posture as the alternative to decrepitude.

I began this journal by explaining that the idea of writing it was inspired by the example of Henry Beetle Hough and his books about Martha's Vineyard. He had and they have great integrity, partly derived from the fact that the permanent community of the Vineyard, outnumbered more than five to one in July and August by the 'Summer People', decided long ago to accommodate them because they realized they had no choice. They took some risks; there are numerous funny stories about the unreliability of local tradesmen. But the stories are not unkind. The Summer People would not have the 'Islanders', as they call them, any other way.

For two or three months of every year, the two communities are daily entwined in mutual respect, bound by mutual affection for their bountiful island, and united by their common determination to protect it. And their relationships are symbolized in a phrase used by the Islanders to tell the summer residents they are part of one community, the only difference between them—as members of that community—being that most of them, because they have to earn a living, are not there most of the time. When summer ends and fall approaches and the Summer People get ready to leave for the mainland, the Islanders say to them: 'We'll miss your lights.' The challenge that faced the two communities on the Vineyard was, and is, enormous: to bind the present with the absent. I think they have succeeded admirably.

In North Norfolk the challenge is smaller: to integrate the local community of North Norfolk People with retiring immigrants and weekenders. If the Vineyarders can do, surely it can be done here too.

It will, however, take vision and leadership. Just this morning I asked a friend of ours, now in her seventies, what she felt about the people from 'away'. Her eyes narrowed a bit as she looked at me and said: 'Don't like 'em .' There's the rub.

Notes on Illustrations

Front cover	Recently constructed footbridge across creek on Warham Marshes looking towards Warham. *(Campbell MacCallum, 1994)*
Frontispiece	Foreshore with driftwood between Wells and Holkham. *(James MacCallum, 1994)*
20th July	Millpond on coast road between Burnham Overy Staithe and Burnham Norton. *(Campbell MacCallum, 1993)*
25th July	International 12 Square Metre Sharpies of Wells Sailing Club racing at Wells. *(Campbell MacCallum, 1993)*
27th July	Les Winter, former landlord of the Lord Nelson at Burnham Thorpe, now retired. *(Campbell MacCallum, 1993)*
28th July	Burnham Overy Staithe Boathouse and hard from the east. *(Campbell MacCallum, 1993)*
30th July	The windmill at Cley from the coast defence bank. *(Campbell MacCallum, 1993)*
1st August	Clinker dinghy on the hard at Brancaster Staithe. *(Campbell MacCallum, 1993)*
3rd August	The astrodome at the site of RAF Langham. *(Campbell MacCallum, 1993)*
4th August	After the harvest at Cockthorpe. *(James MacCallum, 1994)*
5th August	Beach huts on Wells beach. *(Campbell MacCallum, 1993)*
7th August	Burnham Market Street Fair. *(Campbell MacCallum, 1993)*
9th August	Burnham Norton Church. *(Campbell MacCallum, 1993)*
10th August	A 'marsh tide' covers the quay at Blakeney. *(Campbell MacCallum, 1993)*
11th August	A worm digger at Wells. *(Campbell MacCallum, 1993)*
15th August	Binham Priory. *(Campbell MacCallum, 1993)*